Marie Bashkirtseff

Letters of Marie Bashirtseff

Marie Bashkirtseff
Letters of Marie Bashirtseff
ISBN/EAN: 9783337019440

Printed in Europe, USA, Canada, Australia, Japan

Cover: Foto ©ninafisch / pixelio.de

More available books at **www.hansebooks.com**

LETTERS OF
MARIE BASHKIRTSEFF

TRANSLATED BY

MARY J. SERRANO

TRANSLATOR OF "MARIE BASHKIRTSEFF: THE JOURNAL OF A
YOUNG ARTIST," ETC., ETC.

WITH PORTRAITS

CASSELL & COMPANY, Limited
LONDON, PARIS AND MELBOURNE

TRANSLATOR'S PREFACE.

WHEN a name and a personality become the theme of discussion in the columns of newspapers and magazines, on the platforms of debating-societies and lecture-halls, in the drawing-room and the school-room, not in one country or on one continent, but in both hemispheres, when this name and this personality awaken an interest equally keen, equally human, in the breast of the learned and sagacious statesman and of the simple and unsophisticated girl, it is because they are symbolic of some idea or of some quality or combination of qualities of vital and enduring significance to the race. Need it be asked what are the qualities that are inseparably linked with the name and the personality of Marie Bashkirtseff, qualities which have given the Journal she has bequeathed to the world a celebrity unexampled in the literature of recent years? Do they not breathe and burn in her every utterance, are they not manifest in every stroke made by her artist hand; power and sincerity—power not always well-directed, sincerity not always judiciously exercised, but none the less the power that is the condition of all great achievement, the sincerity that is one with the law that keeps the stars in their appointed course.

Power and sincerity are, too, the qualities that most strongly characterize these Letters of Marie Bashkirtseff; but if, as we read the Journal, we think of some bright-hued bird of ethereal lineage, beating its wings, until they bleed, in its wild struggle for freedom, against the bars that stay its skyward flight, reading these Letters we think, rather, of the sun-fed juice of the grape passing through the process of fermentation (here, alas! not to be completed) that is to convert it into the precious wine that invigorates and rejoices and inspires. As it is, Marie Bashkirtseff, fighting against environment, fighting against disease, fighting against fate, has sent from her passionately throbbing girl's heart a cry that will re-echo through the ages—the cry of spirit struggling to cast off the bonds of matter; the cry of Genius proclaiming, in its bonds, its right to stand among the gods.

INTRODUCTION.

Last winter I went to pay my respects to a Russian lady of my acquaintance who was passing through Paris, and who was stopping with Madame Bashkirtseff at her hotel in the Rue Ampère.

I found there a very sympathetic company of middle-aged ladies and young girls, all speaking French perfectly, with that slight accent which gives to our language, when spoken by Russians, an indescribable softness.

In this charming circle, with its pleasant surroundings, I received a cordial welcome. But scarcely was I seated near the "samovar," a cup of tea in my hand, when my attention was arrested by a large portrait of one of the young ladies present—a perfect likeness, freely and boldly treated, with all the *fougue* of a master's brush. "It is my daughter Marie," said Madame Bashkirtseff to me, "who painted this portrait of her cousin."

I began by saying something complimentary. I could not go on. Another canvas, and another, and still another attracted me, revealing to me an exceptional artist. I was charmed by one picture after the other. The drawing-room walls were covered with them, and at each one of my exclamations of delighted surprise, Madame Bashkirtseff repeated to me, with a tone in her voice of tenderness rather than of pride, " It is my daughter Marie "—or, " It is my daughter's."

At this moment Mlle. Bashkirtseff appeared. I saw her but once. I saw her only for an hour. I shall never forget her. Twenty-three years old, but she appeared much younger. Rather short, but with a perfect figure; an oval face exquisitely modeled, golden hair, dark eyes kindling with intelligence—eyes consumed by the desire to see and to know everything—a firm mouth, tender and thoughtful; nostrils quivering like those of a wild horse of the Ukraine.

At the first glance Mlle. Bashkirtseff gave me the rare impression of being possessed of strength in gentleness, dignity in grace. Everything in this adorable young girl betrayed a superior mind. Beneath her womanly charms, she had a truly masculine will of iron, and one was reminded of the gift of Ulysses to the young Achilles—a sword hidden within the garments of a woman.

She replied to my congratulations in a frank and well-modulated voice— without false modesty acknowledging her high ambitions, and—poor child! already with the finger of death upon her—her impatience for fame.

In order to see her other works, we all went upstairs to her studio. There was this extraordinary young girl entirely "in her element."

The large hall was divided into two rooms. The studio proper, where the light streamed through the large sash, and a darker corner heaped up with papers and books. In the one she worked, in the other she read.

By instinct I went straight to the *chef-d'œuvre*—to that " Meeting " which at the last *Salon* had engrossed so much attention. A group of little Parisian street boys, talking seriously together, undoubtedly planning some mischief, before a wooden fence at the corner of a street. It *is* a *chef-d'œuvre*, I maintain. The faces and the attitudes of the children are strikingly real. The glimpse of meager landscape expresses the sadness of the poorer neighborhoods.

At the Exhibition, before this charming picture, the public had with an unanimous voice bestowed the medal on Mlle. Bashkirtseff, who had been already " mentioned " the year before. Why was this verdict not confirmed by the jury? Because the artist was a foreigner? Who knows? Perhaps because of her wealth? This injustice made her suffer, and she endeavored —the noble child!—to avenge herself by redoubling her efforts.

In one hour I saw there twenty canvases commenced; a hundred designs —drawings, painted studies, the cast of a statue, portraits which suggested to me the name of Frans Hals, scenes made from life in the open streets; notably one large sketch of a landscape —the October mist on the shore, the trees half stripped, big yellow leaves strewing the ground. In a word, works in which is incessantly sought, or more often asserts itself, the sentiment of the sincerest and most original art, and of the most personal talent.

Notwithstanding this, a lively curiosity impelled me to the dark corner of the studio, where I saw numerous volumes on shelves and scattered over a work-table. I went closer and looked at the titles. They were the great works of the greatest intellects. They were all there in their own languages—French, Italian, English, and German; Latin also, and even Greek, and they were not "library books," either, as the Philistines call them, "show books," but well-thumbed volumes, read, re-read, and pored over. A copy of Plato, open at a sublime passage, was on the desk.

Before my visible astonishment Mlle. Bashkirtseff lowered her eyes, as if confused at the fear that I might think her a "blue stocking," while her mother proudly kept on telling me of her daughter's encyclopædic learning, and pointed out to me manuscripts black with notes, and the open piano at which her beautiful hands interpreted all kinds of music.

Evidently annoyed by the expression of maternal pride, the young girl laughingly interrupted the conversation. It was time for me to leave, and moreover for a moment I experienced a vague apprehension, a sort of alarm —I can scarcely call it a presentiment.

Before that pale and ardent young girl I thought of some extraordinary hot-house plant, beautiful and fragrant beyond words, and in my heart of hearts a sweet voice murmured, "It is too much!"

Alas! it was indeed too much. A few months after my one visit to the Rue Ampère I received the sinister notice, bordered with black, informing me that Mlle. Bashkirtseff was no more. She had died at twenty-three years of age, having taken a cold while making a sketch in the open air. Once again I visited the now desolate house. The stricken mother, a prey to a devouring and arid grief, unable to shed tears, showed me, for the second time, in their old places, the pictures and the books. She spoke to me for a long time of her poor dead child, revealing the tenderness of her heart, which her intellect had not extinguished. She led me, convulsed by sobs, even to the bed-chamber, before the little iron bedstead, the bed of a soldier, upon which the heroic child had fallen asleep forever. . . . .

But why try to influence the public? In the presence of the works of Marie Bashkirtseff, before that harvest of hopes wilted by the breath of death, every one would surely experience, with an emotion deep as my own, the same profound melancholy as would be inspired by edifices crumbling before their completion, or new ruins scarcely risen from the ground, which flowers and ivy have not yet covered. . . . .

TABLE OF CONTENTS.

	PAGE
Translator's Preface,	v
Introduction,	ix
To Her Aunt,	1
To Her Cousin,	3
To Mlle. B——,	4
To Her Aunt,	7
To Mlle. Colignon,	11
To The Same,	15
To The Same,	16
To Her Mother,	18
To Mlle. X——,	19
To Her Aunt,	20
To Her Cousin,	23
To Her Aunt,	32
To Her Aunt,	35
To The Same,	37
To Her Mother,	38
To Her Grandfather,	43
To Her Brother,	50
To Her Aunt,	52
To The Same,	54
To Her Father,	55
To Her Aunt,	57
To The Same,	60
To Mlle. Colignon,	61

TABLE OF CONTENTS.

	PAGE
To The Same,	64
To Her Mother,	66
To The Same,	68
To Mlle. Colignon,	71
To Mlle. X——,	74
To Her Brother,	77
To Mme. R——,	80
To Her Aunt,	84
To The Marquis of C——,	86
To M. ——,	89
To M. de M——,	93
To The Same,	95
To Mlle. Colignon,	98
To M. de M——,	103
To The Same,	105
To Mlle. B——,	107
To The Same,	110
To Her Mother,	111
To The Same,	114
To The Same,	119
To M. ——,	123
To Mlle. Colignon,	124
To Her Brother,	126
To M. X——,	130
To Her Brother,	132
To A—— M——,	137
To M. Julian,	146
To Her Brother,	150
To Princess K——,	158
To M. X——,	161
To M. Julian,	166

	PAGE
To Her Father,	. 171
To M. B——,	174
To The Same,	. 177
To The Same,	180
To M. Julian,	. 182
To Her Mother,	190
To Mlle. Colignon,	. 192
To Her Mother,	195
To The Same,	. 196
To The Same,	197
To M. Julian,	. 199
To M. B——,	210
To M. Julian,	. 212
To Mlle. ——,	220
To Mlle. ——,	. 222
To Mlle. ——,	227
To M. B——,	. 233
To M. Alexander D——,	235
To The Same,	. 238
To M. ——,	241
To Her Brother,	. 244
To Mlle. Canrobert,	247
To Her Mother,	. 251
To M. B——,	252
To Mlle. ——,	. 253
To The Same,	256
To Her Brother,	. 258
To M. ——,	261
To M. E——,	. 268
To M. de M——,	269
To The Same.	. 272

	PAGE
To The Same,	277
To The Same,	284
To The Same,	287
To The Same,	292
To Baron Saint-Amand,	295
To Her Brother,	298
To M. Henry Houssaye,	302
To M. Edmond de Goncourt,	304
To M. Emile Zola,	307
To M. ———,	310
To M. Tony Robert-Fleury,	321
To M. Sully-Prudhomme,	322
To The Same,	325
To M. Julian,	326
Appendix,	330

LETTERS OF MARIE BASHKIRTSEFF.
1868–1874.

To her Aunt.

JULY 30, 1868.[1]

Dear Aunt Sophie:

How are you and my uncle? Yesterday we had *tableaux vivants*. The first tableau represented the four seasons. Dina was Winter; I, Spring; Sophie Kavérine, Autumn, and Mlle. Élise, Summer. In the second tableau were Dina and Catherine, Sophie's sister. Dina represented Psyche look-

[1] Marie Bashkirtseff was at this time not quite eight years old. She was born on the 11th of November, 1860.

ing at Cupid asleep, and Catherine represented Cupid. Dina wore her hair hanging loose about her shoulders. She looked very pretty. In the third tableau Paul and I took part. I was the Goddess of Flowers and Paul the God of Fruits. In the fourth, Dina appeared as a Naiad; she wore a white robe and was seated among rushes; in her hands and under her feet were river grasses and rushes; her gown was embroidered with white crystal beads that looked like drops of water; through her hair, which hung down her back, white crystal beads were scattered. Come to us at Tcherniakovka; we miss you. All are well and all send you love.

    Your niece,
    Moussia Bashkirtseff.

To her Cousin.

TCHERNIAKOVKA,
February 20, 1870.

Dear Étienne:

I thank you for the drawing and the letters. I am getting on pretty well in my studies. I send you my drawing; but do not show it to any one, because it is badly done. After your departure I made a great many drawings, and some of them are rather good. I don't think we shall go abroad very soon; we may do so, however, one of these days; mamma says we are to set out in a week.

My aunt is gone to her estate with Paul, which is the reason Paul does not write to you. Your sister Dina sends you her love; according to her custom, she does not write; but she remembers your commission. I will bring you a gun-case from abroad; or, rather, write and tell me what you would like me to bring you. But write soon, for in a fortnight at farthest we set out. Be sure and write to me what you would like me to bring you; if we do not go, I will write to you again. *Excuse this bad paper. Mamma sends you three rubles; and I beg you to work hard at school.

Your Devoted Cousin.

To Mlle. B.

September 6, 1873.

My Dear Friend:

To-day for the first time I spoke Italian. Poor Michelletty (my teacher) came near either fainting or throwing himself out of the window with delight at hearing me speak Italian. I can now say that I speak Russian, French, English, and Italian, and I am learning German and Latin; I am studying seriously.

The day before yesterday I took my first lesson in natural philosophy.

Ah, I am very well satisfied with myself!

What a great happiness that is!

How are your studies progressing? Write to me, I beg of you.

I received the Derby. The races at Baden! How I should like to be there! But no, I would not; I must study; and it was with a weight on my heart that I read about the running of X——'s horses. I regained my composure with some difficulty and consoled myself, saying, "Let us study, let us study; our time will come, if God wills it!"

The only hour I have free is the breakfast hour, and they generally choose that time to tease me about X——, and I blush, as I do at everything. Mamma takes my part, saying, ' Why will you always tease her about that X——?"

Mamma was very good to-day. In the end I really believe I shall grow fond of her.

She chatted and laughed and told us stories of her girlhood, and recited verses for us.

Yesterday, at the French lesson, I read sacred history and the Ten Commandments. God says we must not make to ourselves the image of anything that is in the heavens above. The Greeks and the Romans were in error; they were idolaters who worshiped statues and paintings. I am very far from following their example. I believe in God, our Saviour, and the Virgin, and I honor some of the saints, not all, for some of them are manufactured, like plum-cake.

God forgive me for this way of thinking, if it be wrong, but to my simple mind that is how things appear and I cannot speak otherwise than as I feel. Are you pleased with my letter?

Good-by.

To her Aunt.

SPA, Sunday, July 5, 1874.

Dear Aunt:

I promised to write to you, and here

is my letter. I still go out arm in arm with mamma. Yesterday evening I sang at our house and they all came running in from the Casino to hear me. Paul told me he could hear me at the Hotel de Flandre.

Why do we detest some people without knowing why? I was at peace when P—— and her mother came, and now I would like to run away. They are good, amiable, and not stupid, but I cannot bear them.

We went to see the grotto at Spa; I do not know how to describe it to you, and yet how great a pleasure it would be to me, later on, to come across a good description (I will note it all down in my journal) of what I saw! I know that I admired it greatly; but I am sure that there are much more beautiful grottoes in the neighborhood.

not to speak of other countries, where there are marvels beside which this grotto would be as nothing. *And then it is an insult to works of supreme beauty to impose our approbation on them.*

I walked with M. G——, although it was drizzling. I arrived wet and spattered with mud. Mamma was in despair.

The coming back was delightful; at a village where he stopped, G—— took a white coverlet from one of the beds and a rug from the floor. He gave the rug to the others and wrapped the quilt around me. I laughed and admired the boldness of G——. He laughed, too, and compared us to Paul and Virginia.

Count Dönhoff and little B—— K—— were presented to us, and Count D. Basilevsky,—a brother of the Princess Souvaroff,—mamma, Dina, and I went to the races. We had the best seats. Count Basilevsky sat with us. They say he admires mamma, and do you know, dear aunt, what he said? He said, "The daughter is not bad, but she cannot be compared to the mother." Mamma talks of nothing but me; she relates all my childish sayings—the same things over and over again, you know. She still remembers that when she came back from the Crimea (I was two years old at the time) she said to me, on account of some childish frolic or other, "Marie is naughty." And I said to my nurse (for, as you know, I was not weaned until I was three and a half years old) "Marthe, let us go away from here; mamma does not know Marie." Goodby, I send my love to all. I am rosy and fair, and I am very well.

1875.

To Mlle. Colignon.[1]

My Dear Friend:

What a frightful journey.[2] We got out at Vinenbruck, walked for twenty minutes, and reached the place of our destination—a few houses between two mountains—at half past one o'clock. You could never form an idea of the profound quiet that reigns in this place. I think a tomb would be more lively. My mother was enchanted, and I was delighted to see her again. I

[1] Her governess.

[2] Marie Bashkirtseff made her first journey to Schlangenbad at this time,

told her all that had happened since her departure. When I had told her all there was to tell I became tired of the place; there is not a soul here to interest one. I sing and my voice produces the usual effect. They go out walking here bareheaded; every one speaks to every one; *requiem delectabile*. The country is wild,—wilder than in Russia,—melancholy, hateful!

When I think (and I think of it often) that we have only one life, I reproach myself for spending my time in this land of sausages.

A black felt hat, of a charming style, a dark blue cloth princesse gown made very tight over the hips, with a short train, the train gathered up at the side, like a riding-habit; yellow leather shoes with buckles, a fresh face, a regal port (as mamma says), a graceful walk. On seeing me alight, Dina cried out, " I did not know you ; you look like an old-fashioned picture." I asked Dina to take me through the town ; it is not a town but resembles, rather, the park of a château. The scenery is enchanting ; on all sides are hills covered with foliage, balconies with balustrades, rustic bridges, mountains, fields—all truly charming. But no one leans over the balustrades, the walks are deserted, the picturesque terraces deserted also. I complain loudly of this, while I admire all these beauties. On one occasion I was saying that I was bored, when I heard a step behind me ; I turned round and saw a person who was evidently thinking what I had just said; we entered into conversation, when lo!—" Turn quickly," she cried, "and you shall see!" I turned and I saw—a pink and white pig, led by a ribbon. At seven we went down to the dairy; it was charming.

The path, ascending and descending, is enchanting. Schlangenbad is a delightful garden—no squares, no streets; here and there are neat and simple little houses. I speak very little German; I speak a language of my own, adding on *irt* to all the French words. Everybody laughs and mimics me. Mamma has presented me to Princess M———. I complained of being bored and the princess placed at my service a Russian military *attaché*, who is staying here, whose name I do not know.

I shall resign myself to going to bed

early and getting up with the chickens; that will be good for my health.

I cannot tell you how greatly I regret that you are not here with us, it would be of so much benefit to you. Good-by.

To the Same.

My Dear Friend:

The ancients were wrong in making Love a boy. It is the woman who loves. If one could have a second self, I should like to be that self, in order to render homage to my first self only because she renders homage to Love.

What of the woman who loves you blindly? Is she appreciated, even if she adores you? Yes, by commonplace people. But if this woman stands erect before you, and then throws herself at your feet, you comprehend her grandeur, the grandeur of her love. And it is not because she *thus humiliates* herself that she is great, but because she elevates and ennobles you. Where is the man who would not feel himself a god in the presence of adoration like this, and who would not, consequently, understand such a woman and render himself her equal! Goodby.

To the Same.

My Dear Friend:

Are you still at Allevard; and how is your health? Where do you suppose I am to-day? At the Hotel Planz at Schlangenbad? Not at all. I am at the Grand Hotel at Paris, and if you had looked at my letter before opening it, you would have known it from the envelope. I am a naughty girl; I left my mother saying I was delighted to depart with my uncle. That made her feel unhappy, and people do not know how much I love her, and they judge me by appearances. Oh! according to appearances I am not very affectionate. The thought of seeing my aunt again fills my mind completely! Poor aunt, who is so lonely without me! Poor mamma, whom I have deserted! Good Heavens! what am I to do? I cannot cut myself in two!

On Friday I left Schlangenbad. At five o'clock on Saturday I alighted at the door of the Grand Hotel, where my aunt was waiting for me. At the

French frontier I breathed freely for the first time since I left France.

With love.

To her Mother.

PARIS, GRAND HOTEL.

Dear Mamma:

We arrived at five this morning at the Grand Hotel, and though it is now only six, I am writing to you, which proves my promptness.

I breathed freely for the first time in a fortnight when I saw France again. I am in splendid health; I feel that I am beautiful; it seems to me that I shall succeed in all I undertake; everything smiles on me, and I am happy, happy, happy!

I send you a kiss. Good-by.

Take care of yourself, mamma; write to me and come soon.

———

To Mlle X——.

PARIS, September 1.

My Dear Berthe:

I answer your letter from Paris, where I have been for the last three days. My mother, who remained at Schlangenbad, forwarded it to me. Your mother is very good to think of me, and I am impatient to make her acquaintance. I am here with my aunt, Madame Romanoff—I think you have met her. How I should like to spend some days in the same city with you—we could at least see each other. It is unsatisfactory to meet each other two or three times a year, exchange a few words, and then be again, the one at one end of the world, the other at the other.

Let us always write to each other. Since our first sojourn abroad, when we knew each other as children, I have felt attracted toward you, and something tells me that we shall one day be more closely united than we can be now.

We are at the Grand Hotel, No. 281.

Good-by for the present, my dear; think of me as I think of you. Good-by.

To her Aunt.

PARIS.

Mme. Romanoff, Olga, Marie,—every-one, in short:

I write according to my promise, and

in the first place, I am going to declare that it is not at all warm, as my aunt has said, but delightfully cool — beautiful weather in fact. I have visited all my tradespeople, who are real angels, and not as dear as I had thought. K—— is with us and is wonderfully useful. Yesterday and the day before we went to the Bois. There was an immense crowd there, fashionable, as usual.

Your brother, beautiful Euphrosine, has an adorable horse and carriage and plays the beau here. He turned a somersault when he saw me. That ape L—— is here too, as are also a number of other people whom we met at Nice and elsewhere. Only, I am in want of money. That is the chief thing. Who the deuce invented that vile thing? How happy they were at

Sparta to have only leather money—money made from an ox-hide. I economize wonderfully, but notwithstanding all my economy, money *deficit*.

I manage my affairs better than I had thought I could. I must accustom myself to do this. One is very unhappy when one can do nothing for one's self.

My greatest torment is to have to go rambling about with Aunt Marie. They have all just left the house to go to the Bon Marché. I have stayed at home and am shut up in my room, which I like a hundred times better than running about the shops.

To her Cousin.

PARIS, GRAND HOTEL.

Dear Dina:

I have met with an adventure! I was standing on the balcony of the reading-room, waiting for my aunt, when I heard behind me a chorus of praises of my person, my figure. These praises proceeded from a group of gentlemen seated behind me. It is true that in my princesse robe of gray batiste my figure is divine, that is the word (you have said so yourself); my golden hair was simply dressed. I cannot describe it to you, but the braids fell half-way down my back; this was not all; among the group were some Brazilians who watched me and followed me; this was not all; there was a charming young Englishman who seemed to be taken with me; this was not all; there was a frightful blond Russian who pursued me; this was not all, and even if I should think this were all, there are a great many other fools of whom I shall not take the trouble to speak. Even the women look at me and admire my toilets, which are astonishingly simple and surprisingly *chic*. Read my letter to mamma; it will please her; it will cure her; poor mamma!

A victoria with a pair of horses was brought to the door and we drove out.

In the Bois the carriages were four abreast; we were almost crushed to death. I was going to express my wonder at the ugliness of the men when I saw a familiar figure approach.

I tried to recollect where I had seen him before—one sees so many people, so many faces that the sight grows weary and the mind confused. The person saluted me and I saw smiling on me the countenance of the stupid Em.

At the second turn the surprising but stupid personage approached the vehicle and in his harsh voice, with his Nicene accent, uttered these remarkable words, "Where are you staying?" "At the Grand Hotel," answered my aunt. "Very good." As for me, I did not even look at him.

I don't know what to attribute the revulsion of feeling to, but before everything seemed dark to me and now everything seems rose-colored. We returned just in time for the hotel dinner. To the left were the men I called the Brazilians; to the right, in the reading room, was the handsome Englishman, who came to the window twenty times to have an excuse to look at me. I saw him glance at me each time from out of the corner of his eye, from behind the paper he pretended to be reading.

Oh, truly, I am not worth all this trouble! I went to my room and began to write. A knock came to the door; the chambermaid handed me a card—De M——'s. I told her to show him in. It was Remy, alone, without his father. I looked at his hat on the table, at his black hair, and an idea struck me. "Sit down," I said, "with your back toward the door, and do not turn around when my aunt comes in; I want her to think you are some one else." And our talk was interrupted at every moment by our bursts of laughter; I pictured to myself the expression on my aunt's face when she should see him.

Remy assures me that he has not changed in all these four years.

"How many girls have you been in love with, meantime?" I asked him. "Not one! I swear it!" I doubted, he protested; I laughed, he sighed. It is pleasant to keep the friends of one's childhood. In those days, as you know, he was a hundred times more of a flirt than I. Now I am an old woman and he is a child. He ventured to ask me if I had changed.

"Not at all," I anwered. "I am still the same. I am not in love with you; that goes without saying."

I meant that I had never been so

But why destroy people's illusions? (It will be three years still before he finishes his studies.) He shook his head and stammered some words which signified, " Oh, of course not ; I never dared to think otherwise." " But," I continued, "I am your friend."

My aunt entered the room, and I burst out laughing when I saw her face, at once astonished, smiling, and severe. She assumed a ceremonious air, but Remy turned around, and her expression changed instantaneously. "Oh, oh, oh ! what a delightful surprise!"

In the Bois[1] there were so many people from Nice that for a moment I fancied myself in Nice.

[1] The end of this letter is to be found, slightly varied, in the journal of Marie Bashkirtseff.

It is September, and Nice is so beautiful in September! I thought of last year; my morning walks there with my dogs, the cloudless sky, the silvery sea. Here there is neither morning nor evening; in the morning they are sweeping, in the evening the innumerable lights irritate my nerves. I am completely lost here. I cannot tell the east from the west, while there I feel so perfectly at home! One is in a nest, as it were, surrounded by mountains, neither too high nor too arid. On three sides one is sheltered, as if by one of Laferrière's graceful and comfortable mantles, and in front is an immense window, a limitless horizon, always the same, always new. Ah, I love Nice. Nice is my country. Nice has given me my growth; Nice has given me health and a fresh color. It is so beautiful there; one gets up with the dawn, and to the left one sees the sun rise behind mountains that stand out clearly against a silvery blue sky, so soft and vapory that one can scarcely breathe for joy. At midday the sun faces my window; it is warm, but the air is not warm; there is that incomparable breeze that always keeps the atmosphere cool. Everything seems wrapped in slumber. There is not a soul to be seen on the promenade but three or four old men of the place, asleep on benches. There I am alone; there I can breathe freely; there is something to admire, something to awaken the emotions. What am I telling you? Things you already know; but as I am in the mood I will go on.

And at night the same sky, the same sea, the same mountains. But at night all is black or deep blue. And when the moon throws across the water a broad pathway of light, like a fish with diamond scales, and I am seated at my window, tranquil and alone, I ask for nothing more, and I prostrate myself in thankfulness before God! Ah, no! you cannot understand what I want to say, you will never understand it, because you have never felt it. No, this is not what I mean, but it makes me desperate when I try to express what I feel. It is as if I had a nightmare and had not the strength to cry out.

And then, words can never give an idea of real life. How describe the freshness, the perfume of memory!

One may invent, one may create, but one cannot copy. It is in vain to feel when one writes; only commonplace words are the result—woods, mountains, sky, moon, etc., etc.

Write me all the news from Schlangenbad, and come soon.

To her Aunt.

PARIS.

My Very Dear Aunt:

Do not torment yourself needlessly and do not indulge in gloomy forebodings. Everything is going on admirably, except the disposition of my august mother, who is out of humor from morning till night, and who economizes to such an extent that it is terrible. My august mother proposed to do away with breakfast—fancy that, to do away with breakfast! This was atrocious; but I am good-natured; I did not get angry, and the proposition has remained a proposition.

The whole world is in Paris, from the Queen of Spain to A——.

We have seen several hotels. There is one in the Champs-Élysées, standing by itself, with a little garden, stables, and a coach-house, three servants' rooms, eight bedrooms, three parlors, a dining-room, a winter garden, cellars, kitchen, bath-room, servants' hall, etc., etc. It is not a very large house, and if we hire it, it will be necessary to add two or three rooms to it. It is only in Paris that one can live; everywhere else one vegetates. When I think that I live in Nice, I am ready to knock my head against the wall. And to think that we have bought a house at Nice! How horrid! I know that I shall be ridiculed for what I say, but I don't care. I say what I say, and I know what I know. To live anywhere but here is to lose one's time, one's money, one's beauty, one's health — everything in short. Every living man of sense will say that I am right. How is papa's health? Embrace him for me. I intend to win 2,000,000 rubles, and then I will show you from whom I am descended.

> I am the daughter of Madame Angot, etc.

When I think that we are selling in Russia to buy in Nice! But this is nonsense.

In fine, since the affair is begun finish it; pay for the house at Nice and then we can try to sell it, if we find a purchaser. Pray buy no furniture, as we can order it here; it is not worth while to spend money for this Nicene barracks.

I send a hundred kisses. Have Prater shaved and washed.

P. S.—I inclose my photograph as *Mignon*, for the *tableaux vivants*.

To her Aunt.

EPISTLE TO MY AUNT ASKING FOR MONEY.

The eldest of the Graces three
Is plunged in direst misery!
If your charitable soul,
Of great things capable, her dole
Will pity, as I hope, believe

That every franc you shall receive
Again with interest, when I'm queen.
My soul, that shrinks from all things
   mean,
And my splendor-loving heart
Lose their freshness, like a tart,
In this pitiful hotel.
Wherefore, most advisable,
My drooping spirits to revive,
In the Bois a daily drive
At the evening hour to be,
Dear aunt, you surely will agree.
But gowns, for this, and carriages
Are indispensable, and these,
With an empty exchequer,
How, alas! provide? Give ear,
I pray, to my petition, then,
And send me money, which again
I will return, when I am queen.

To the Same.

Paris.

It rained all the morning.

Ah, aunt, if you could send me a little of the vile metal!

In truth, I cannot understand how there can be people who might live in Paris and yet prefer to vegetate in Nice!

If you only knew how beautiful Paris is! At Laferrières, Caroline is gone to the waters; the tall, thin girl fills her place, and not badly; at least with her, I can do as I choose.

Ah, aunt, do then send me some money,

> For I am in dire distress,
> And my heart, and my heart,
> Sad and anxious thoughts oppress!

Not to go every day to the Bois is

to die of *ennui;* you know well that I detest running about the boulevards and the shops. My only pleasure is to go breathe the pure air of the country, to inhale the sweet odors of the Bois, to admire nature—the nature of the carriages and the dresses.

Ah, aunt, do then send me some money,

> For I am in dire distress,
> And my heart, and my heart.
> Sad and anxious thoughts oppress!

God keep you, my friends. We, by the grace of God,

MARIE.

To her Mother.
FLORENCE.

Dear Mamma :

We alighted at the Hotel de France. Ah, I am used to traveling; I have been doing nothing else for some time past. I am well and happy. What is disagreeable is that we do not know a soul—that we two women, my aunt and myself, are here alone. Well, we must try to make the best of it.

What life! What animation! Songs, cries, on all sides. I feel at my ease here. We are here as if we were in the heart of a wood, in the *selva reggia* of Dante. I know neither where the people are going nor what they are doing. I know nothing, nothing, nothing! But, as a Russian poet says, our happiness consists in our miserable ignorance. He is right. I am ignorant of all that is going on here, and I am almost tranquil. I should take it very ill of the person who would attempt to draw me out of *this miserable ignorance*, who should say to me, "There is a ball there, a fête here." I should want to be there and that would torment me.

It is a lovely moonlight night, and our hotel is situated on the only spot on the banks of the Arno which is not arid and ugly, like the Paillon of Nice. To-morrow we will visit the galleries and the palace!

Ah, how pleasant life is here! We visited the Pitti Palace, and afterward the picture gallery. The picture which struck me most was the "Judgment of Solomon," the figures in mediæval costumes; there are several other pictures as *naïve* as this. You know I have a respect for very old pictures, but this does not prevent me from seeing their defects. There was a Venus with feet so distorted that one might have thought she had been in the habit of wearing high-heeled shoes. My own feet are of a much better shape. There are very beautiful and curious objects in the palace, thousands of them. What I like best are the portraits, because they are not invented, composed, arranged. There is also a curious collection of miniatures. Why do we not dress now as they did in olden times? The present fashions are ugly. You know that I have settled on the style of dress I shall wear, once I am married—it is to be classic—the style of the Empire, or rather, of the *Directoire*—but modest, very modest. There are some charming gowns, draped carelessly, and fastened in front with a belt. Ah, the women of to-day do not know how to dress; the most elegant of them are badly dressed. Well, have patience;

if God grants me grace to do what I wish, you shall see one woman, at least, dressed with some taste.

From the picture gallery we went to the house of Buonarotti, but there was such a crowd that we could see nothing. Afterward we went to the Museo del Pietre D. A superb collection of mosaics! Then to the Galeria del Belorta. I shall not describe it; when you are well we will go there together; besides, it would take a volume to describe it, and the description would give no idea of it. You know I adore painting, sculpture, art, in a word.

Good-by for a while. With love.

To her Grandfather.

FLORENCE,
Wednesday, September 15.

Dear Grandpapa:

We visited the Galeria degli Uffizi, which communicates with the Pitti Palace, of which I saw as much yesterday as it was possible to see in a passing view. To-day I remained in the gallery for an hour and a half; I spent a long time looking at the statues and the busts.

I was disappointed in the head of Alcibiades. I had never pictured him to myself with that bald forehead, that small mouth, showing the teeth; that closely trimmed beard.

Cicero is well enough (don't be uneasy, I do not take him for a Greek);

but that poor Socrates! He did well to study philosophy and converse with his Dæmon. There was nothing else for him to do. How absurdly ugly!

At last I beheld the famous Venus de Medici. This doll was another disappointment. Those narrow shoulders do not arouse my admiration, and the head and the features are like those of all Greek statues. No, this is not Venus, the enchanting goddess, the mother of Love. The mouth is cold; the lips are expressionless; the proportions, indeed, are admirably preserved, but what would be left if the proportions were less perfect! I may be called barbarous, ignorant, arrogant, stupid, but this is my opinion. The Venus of Milo is much more like a Venus.

I passed on to the pictures, and found at last something worthy of the name of Raphael—not a faded, insipid image, like some of his Madonnas; not an Infant Christ that looks as if it were made of *papier maché*, but a lifelike, fresh, beautiful head— *la Fornarina*. Perhaps it is because I understand nothing about the matter, but I prefer this head a thousand times to all his Madonnas put together. "A Woman," by Titian, fair and plump, is admirable as Flora; she reappears in a painting in the Pitti Palace, by Titian, also, representing "Cleopatra Causing Herself to be Bitten by an Asp," in which she is absurd—too fat, too fair, not at all like a Greek-Egyptian. The effects of light in the pictures of Gherardo delle Notti pleased me infinitely. The figures are beautiful and life-like. The large canvas representing the "Shepherds beside the Cradle of Jesus" is superb. Without the hackneyed aureole, the Divine Infant illumines the figures of those who surround him and seems himself made of light. The Virgin Mary lifts up the cloth, uncovering the Infant, and looks at the shepherds with a truly heavenly smile. The faces of these latter are lighted up with an expression of adoration, and those who are nearest shade their eyes with their hands as one does when one is dazzled by the sunlight. All the faces are beautiful and true to nature. It is plain that the painter understood what he was about.

In the French Hall there is a very pretty small portrait by Mignard, and in the Flemish Hall there is a picture by Franz van Myeris which enchanted me on account of its extraordinary delicacy. The more closely one examines it the finer it seems, and the more wonderful the coloring. I mention only the pictures which I noticed particularly; and then I devoted most of my time to the busts of the Roman emperors and the Roman women, Agrippina Poppæa and—I have forgotten her name. Nero is incomparably beautiful.

Marcus Aurelius has a fine, large head.

Titus resembles some one I have seen, whom I cannot remember.

They have just brought us the ticket for the box at the Palliano Theater to-night. They do not give a ticket, but the key of the box and two cards of admission; I have seen this fashion only in Italy.

We leave here to-morrow. The more I see the more I want to see. I can scarcely tear myself away from all these beauties. The Venus de Medici made me very proud. Later we shall visit the Egyptian and Etruscan museums.

Primitive art has its charms, but I do not think, as they say, that Greek sculpture was brought from Egypt.

It is of an entirely different character and then, as I believe, even in the remotest times in Greece there was never anything resembling Egyptian art, as in Egypt there was never, nor is there now, anything at all approaching the magnificence of Greek art.

In Egypt, art has always remained the same—imposing and absurd. I am sorry I cannot better explain what I comprehend so well. Ah, dear grandpapa, if you were only with us! Well, let us leave proud Florence. That *Lanza leggiera piota molt che dipel maculato era caperta*, as the long-nosed Dante says. Here is another long nose.

Let us return, let us return to our own town, the haughty city of Segurana. Once more to the railway carriage! What a pity there were no railroads in the time of Dante! He would certainly have made them one of the punishments of his Inferno. This ill-smelling smoke, this noise, this perpetual shaking!

Good-by for a while. With love.

To her Brother.

NICE.

Dear Paul:

I have just returned from Florence, where aunt took me for a visit. At Monte-Carlo I was already rosy with happiness, and I laughed for joy all the way to Nice. We had telegraphed for the carriage and we found it waiting for us. Instead of undressing I went to see the masons, who are making alterations in the rooms; then I ran upstairs to the second floor, where we are to lodge in the mean time. I am going to tell you everything. When I was in my own room I took off my gown, rushed to my books, and arranged them in the book-cases, and having finished this task, I threw myself on the carpet and spent an hour playing with my two dogs—the only real friends a man can have, even if that man were Socrates himself. *Poi, poi, riposto un poco il corpo lasso, ripressivia per la piaggoginivesta.* But this was not until I had washed myself from head to foot and put on a fine white chemise, a petticoat, and my gray batiste gown, without the bodice, which I changed for a white foulard cape ; you know how becoming that is to me. I shall try to be contented then, and with my books spend agreeably the few days we still have to remain here. Tell me what you are doing ; give me a minute account of your life at Gavronzy. I embrace you and I pity you.

1876.

To her Aunt.

HOTEL DE LONDRES,
 PIAZZA DI SPAGNA,
  ROME, January 3.

Dear Aunt:

At last I am in Rome, after a wretched night spent in a full compartment, on cushions as hard as wood. It was horrible, but it is over, and we are at the Hotel de Londres, Piazza di Spagna. What is atrocious is to have to haggle!

Send Léonie on at once, with whatever things we may have forgotten. I left my note-paper and a box of pens behind. Send them to me. Do not forget my recommendation with respect to the furniture. Be sure to send the telegram about the horses to Alexandre, without changing it. Take care of my dogs.

I am in despair at having forgotten to bid grandpapa good-by, but I was so hurried, there was such noise and confusion! Tell him, dear aunt, that I send him a thousand, thousand embraces, that I kiss his hands, and beg him to forgive my unpardonable negligence.

I have little news as yet to tell you. I have not seen Rome, but it seems to me like a great machine.

We arrived only a couple of hours ago. To-morrow I will write to everybody.

Good-by.

Take care of yourself and come soon,

so that my present companions may return in peace to the city of Catherine Segurana.

A thousand kisses.

To the Same.

Dear Aunt:

I inclose you another letter, which I beg you will stamp and post for me.

We are all well. Instead of remaining in the house, go everywhere, and write and tell me all that is going on at Nice.

Give my love to D—— P—— and T——.

Send Léonie and Fortuné to me. Send me, also, my white parasol, which I think I left at Nice.

Try to come to us as soon as possible.

Bring D—— P—— with you.

I am well, and send you my love.

Good-by.

To her Father.

Hotel de Ville,
    Rome, March 10.

Dear Father:

You have always been prejudiced against me, although I have never done anything to justify such a feeling on your part. I have never lost the love and esteem for you, however, which every well-born girl owes to her father.

I regard it as my duty to consult you on all serious matters, and I am persuaded that you will take the interest in them which they deserve.

I have been asked in marriage by Count B——. Mamma will have already told you of this, but yesterday I also received a proposal from Count A——, the nephew of Cardinal A——.

I consider myself too young to marry, but in any case I ask your advice in the matter, and I hope that you will give it to me. Both the gentlemen I have named are young, rich, and have done all in their power to please me. I regard them both with indifference.

While awaiting an answer to my letter I remain, with the greatest respect and esteem,

Your devoted and obedient daughter.

To her Aunt.

ROME.

Dear Aunt:

Last night at the theater there was a young man who looked at me persistently through his opera-glass, like a fool. I felt inclined to be indignant, but to show anger would be to expose myself to ridicule. I acted with perfect unconcern, pretending to have noticed nothing. There is no one here whom I. like ; this young fellow interested me because he watched me like a fool, and because he was in a box and the friends with whom he was chatting (they had five or six boxes in a row) seemed to be gentlemen of fashion.

In every opera troupe there must be a prima donna, at every *réunion* a *primo* N—— N——. I looked for one all the evening, but in vain.

There were plenty of them, but there was not one who was distinguishable from the rest.

Black eyes, black hair, a pale complexion. The young fellow was separated from us only by two boxes, and he changed his place continually to get a view of my face, impatiently waiting for me to lower my opera-glass so that he might look at me, which he did without ceasing during the whole evening; that is to say, from eight o'clock until midnight.

The exit is very handsome and was crowded with men; you pass between two living walls composed of hundreds of persons, just the same as at Nice, only that at Nice there are comparatively few people, while here it is a pleasure to go out from the opera. I love those human hedges, those hundreds of eyes fixed upon one. And they are very polite here; they make room for one to pass.

The next time I go to the opera, I shall enjoy myself still more, for I now know a great many people by sight.

The evening reminded me of some of the evenings at Nice—less brilliant, but much more home-like; there I am at home, and according to the Russian proverb, "It is pleasant to visit, but it is pleasanter to be at home."

You will see that after three or four visits I shall adore the Apollo, and then to feel those thousands of black eyes all looking at me is a sort of distraction which suits me. I can dispense with looking at others, as long as others look at me, and I like this even better.

Good-by; love to all. Mamma is well and writes to you.

To the Same.

ROME.

Dear Aunt:

I shall begin by saying that my health is excellent.

Reassure yourself, I beg of you; I am rosier than ever.

In the next place, I have a commission to give you.

Send me my old *mousseline de laine* gown with the white braid, and the skirt of the *mousseline de chine* gown, the one trimmed with gold braid.

As for the box from Laferrière, it contains a gown which you must also send me here. Worth is going to send some ball dresses to Nice and you can send them to us immediately to Rome. You must lose no time. We are beginning to get settled in Rome. A thousand kisses. How are matters progressing?

To Mlle. Colignon.

JUNE 13.

My Dear Friend:[1]

I, who would like to live half-a-dozen lives at once, do not live even a quarter of a life. I am held in fetters, but God will have pity on me. I have no

[1] See in the journal of Marie Bashkirtseff, page 81, a fragment which reproduces the ideas expressed in this letter.

strength; I feel as if I must die. It is as I have said, I desire either to acquire all that God has given my mind the power to grasp and to comprehend, in which case I should be worthy of attaining it, or to die. For if God cannot, without injustice to others, grant me everything, he will not have the cruelty to allow an unhappy girl, whom he has endowed with understanding and the ambition to excel in what she understands, to live.

God has not made me such as I am without some purpose. He cannot have given me the power to understand all things in order to torture me by denying me everything. Such a supposition is not in accordance with the nature of God, who is just and merciful.

I must attain what I desire or I must die. He who is afraid, yet goes to meet danger, is braver than he who is not afraid. And the greater the fear the greater the merit. The past lives in memory and is consequently a sort of present. The future does not exist. Let us not try to evade the question by a sophism saying that this instant in which I am writing to you is already past; by the present we understand to-day, to-morrow, a week hence. This leads me to say that one should take no thought for the future, regret nothing. Do we live for the future?

And do we gain anything by making the present unhappy, in order to enjoy the hope of future happiness? Do not scold me, and good-by.

To the Same.

My Dear Friend:

I am happy in your happiness; one can never learn good news too soon. Is it a merit to be calm when calmness is in one's nature? I am both sad and enraged. *Nothing remains to me* but the remembrance of a great disappointment, and if I am disgusted, it is to see that my life has been a failure. You know *I had a sort of pride in thinking I was going to make my life glorious and beautiful. I regarded it with the selfish affection of a painter who is working on a picture which he desires to make his masterpiece.* Bear well in mind the words that are underlined; in them you have the principal cause of all my troubles and the expression and the exact explanation of all my vexations—past, present, and to come. I am so peculiarly constituted that I regard my life as something apart from me, and on this life I have fixed all my ambition and all my hopes; if it were not for this I should be indifferent to everything. Remember well, then, remember well these words, my dear friend, they explain everything, and spare me the trouble of expressing and explaining my feelings.

I look pretty to-day. Nothing beautifies so greatly as the consciousness of being beautiful. One should pay the strictest attention to little things, for life is made up of them, and one becomes worse than the animals if one neglects them. I am becoming a philosopher. Good-by.

To her Mother.

JULY 3.

Dear Mamma:[1]

What am I? Nothing. What do I want? Everything.

Let me rest my spirit, fatigued by all these bounds toward the infinite, and let us return to A——. Ah, still thinking of him, a boy, a miserable creature!

No, the principal thing is that I must leave my journal at home! I am taking Pietro's letter with me; I will tell you why; I have just re-read it. He is unhappy! Why, then, has he so little spirit? It is all very well for me to speak in this way, in my exception-

---

[1] See the journal of Marie Bashkirtseff, pages 87 and 88. The same ideas are there repeated and sometimes in the same words.

ally independent position (for you indulge me greatly), but him!— And those Romans—there are no people like them. Poor Pietro!

My future glory prevents me from thinking about him seriously; it seems to reproach me for the thoughts I devote to him.

No, Pietro is only a diversion—*a strain of music in which to drown the lamentations of my soul.* And yet I reproach myself for thinking of him, since he can be of no use to me. He cannot even be the first rung of the ladder that leads to fame.

Ah, dear mamma, you cannot understand me, but I must tell you what I feel, all the same.

If I were remarkable for anything, I should be famous—but remarkable for what? Singing and painting! Are they not enough? The one is present triumph; the other eternal glory!

For both alike it would be necessary to go to Rome, and to be able to study one must have a tranquil mind. I should have to take my father with me, and to do this I should have to go to Russia. Well, then, I will go there!

You are now in grief, but we shall one day triumph over all our enemies and we shall yet be happy, I promise you.

Good-by. With love.

To the Same.

PARIS, July.

Dear Mamma:

The heat is stifling. We have been

shopping, and we went to see our carriages,—which are very handsome. We have not yet met any one we know, and then this is the most abominable season in Paris, although there is a good deal going on.

The day after to-morrow I am going to consult the somnambulist, and I will write the result to you.

I hope you will not grieve too much on account of my absence. Have the white curtains of my room folded and remember what I said about the carpet.

I shall soon return—in three months, or perhaps less. And then, there is no attraction for me in Russia, nothing requires my presence there. I shall go because things are progressing badly, and I hope to arrange matters satisfactorily.

Amuse yourself, and be sure and go to Schlangenbad; take care of your health, and write me kind letters.

Aunt is well; she sends you her love.

Good-by; take care of yourself. Love to you, grandpapa, and Dina. Write.

1877.

To Mlle. Colignon.

My Dear Friend:

B——, whom you admire so much, came this morning to bring some songs for Soria to sing to-night, in order that he should not have to come carrying his bundle under his arm.

I went out with mamma, and afterward I went through the rooms to see if they had brought the flowers and if all the arrangements were to my taste. We had a few guests at dinner. I must confess that I did not find them very amusing, so that I soon retired to my room, where I spent about an hour reading. I had scarcely gone down again when G—— arrived and immediately afterward B——, Diaz de Soria, and Rapsaïd.

I took possession of Rapsaïd, who is the most celebrated amateur tenor here, and who is in great demand, as it appears. (He is ugly, intelligent, and a Belgian.) While Soria chatted with mamma, he seized the first opportunity that presented itself to come over and take the other seat of the *tête-à-tête* on which I was sitting, and *attacked* me— that is the word.

With his olive complexion, black beard, bald head, and large, brilliant Arab eyes, it was the most natural thing in the world that he should be captivated by my fair hair and white skin. Instead of going into ecstasies and begging him to sing, I said that I never begged anything; that if he had a mind to sing, he would sing of his own accord. He sang divinely. Until the departure of Soria, B——, and Rapsaïd, there was a brilliant succession of *bon mots*, songs, and bursts of laughter.

The most flattering things were said to me. A—— would like to see me entering the ball-room of the Tuileries in state; the general compared me to one of the Vestal Virgins, the others to —I don't know what; Soria to Galatea. Animated by all this, and fearing that I was neglecting the ladies, I returned to them, and we installed ourselves in the little smoking-room, where we chatted and laughed about a hundred amusing things, until it was half-past twelve. Nice evidently wishes that my last impression of it shall be a pleasant one.

I embrace you and regret that you are not with us.

Write to me and take care of your health.

To Mlle. X——.

NICE.

My Dear Friend:

There is no occasion for me to conceal my sentiments for the young man you mention, because he never made any impression upon me, because I have never liked him, and because if he had never chanced to notice me, I might have lived next door to him for a hundred years without even being aware of his existence.

As for serious fancies, I have only had two in my life—the first, when I was a child of thirteen, for the Duke of H——.

I speak of this sentiment from recollection only, for the feeling itself I have long forgotten; and I suppose there was in it a good deal of fictitious enthusiasm, of which I had, at that time, *abundance*, and for everything, and which I did not know what to do with.

The second was for Count de L——; but it was not at the races that I conceived this fancy for him; at the races the only impression he produced upon me was that of a handsome boy.

The day after, when I was at the Toledo with X——, I perceived that he had *some style*. And at the railway station, when we were leaving Naples, I completely lost my heart.

You remember what I said that evening—I fell in love with him the instant I saw him looking in at me through the window of the railway carriage.

I cannot describe my sensations; such feelings are indescribable and incomprehensible.

I saw him again afterward, but without experiencing any other emotion than that which was produced by the recollection of the first strange electric shock. On this last occasion it was not that he himself made any impression upon me, but I suddenly remembered my former feeling for him and I felt it again, in the recollection, almost as strongly as I had felt it on the original occasion.

And the same thing happens now whenever I think of him, although indeed I hardly ever think of him.

To her Brother.

NICE.

Dear Paul:

Yesterday Faure sang in "Faust" before a brilliant audience. We arrived before the rising of the curtain—my aunt, Dina, I, the general, and M——, and, shortly afterward, Marquis R——.

From the first moment to the last I felt happy, without knowing why. I even made some *bon mots*, which might have some success if—but no one will think of repeating them. Well, they will certainly be more likely to be repeated than if any one else had made them. Several other persons came; the crowd was uncomfortable, and B—— slipped away.

But before anything else, let me tell you that I am enchanted, charmed, captivated by the playing, the singing, and the face of Faure. Yes, just so, of this actor. He was not an actor, he was not a singer, he was not a perfect *Mephistopheles*—he was Satan himself. Costume, manners, face, the illusion was complete—devilish subtlety; pitiless, diabolic raillery; cynical and flippant philosophy.

Side by side with this perfection of art, I saw what I shall doubtless never see again—a *Marguerite* who did not sing. That is too much, you will say. It is true. At first I thought she was agitated, frightened; and when she began the air of the "King of Thule," I trembled and hid myself in the corner of the box as frightened and ashamed as if I myself were the singer. She uttered a moan, murmured a few sounds, shrieked—it was so bad that they did not even deign to hiss.

What delightful hours those were! The box was full of people, which prevented me from falling into one of my gloomy moods. The music was divine, enveloping me like a triple cloak of well-being, which warmed my heart and enchanted me.

During the tiresome parts I laughed and jested with my companions in the box, all of them intellectual people. That night I fancied myself happy, and I prayed on my knees to God to allow my throat to be cured so that I could study singing. For that is true life! The details of "Faust" may please, in a certain way, thanks to the music, but the subject is disgusting. I do not say immoral, hideous; I say *disgusting*.

I wore a gown of a clinging and elastic material that modestly revealed the outlines of my figure; my hair was dressed *à la Psyche*, gathered up at the back of the head in a knot of natural curls. Every one said that my appearance was entirely original—coiffure, costume, figure—I seemed a living statue, and not merely a young lady, like so many others. You should be proud, my dear boy, to have a sister like me.

Enough for to-day.

With love.

To Mme. R——.

NAPLES, April 2.

Your letter delighted me. All that you say is so true that I have thought it a hundred times; only, you overestimate my real worth.

I was worth something once, perhaps, but so much travel has dulled my faculties. I have always suffered from the throat, and it was thought the climate of Naples might prove beneficial to me.

Do not take too seriously what I write to-night; I am in a melancholy mood and consequently everything looks gloomy to me; this happens to everybody.

It makes me happy to think that in a month more we shall be settled in Paris, which I hope we shall never leave.

Cropped ears have their charms for the one who crops them. Scold me well; do not hesitate to say all you wish to me; that will keep me in an almost healthy frame of mind. I am tired myself of idling; your words make me angry with myself, with every one. I should have gone to sleep without your reproaches, which I understand and appreciate. Do you suppose that I have not formed a hundred projects, but to what purpose!

Yesterday I was almost cheerful listening to Pergolesi's "Stabat," which was repeated for the Princess Marguerite, and of which the divine harmonies filled my heart and my ears; to-night I am depressed.

Mamma and Dina are at last at San Carlo. I have remained at home, which has caused a little domestic skirmish in which I have played an entirely passive part. For some time past I have been so sensible and quiet that it is dreadful. I am bored; but what would you have me do there?

I cannot amuse myself by going wild over a fool or even over a man of sense. That sort of amusement has charms for me only as an accessory.

I believe I am writing nonsense; take from my letter only what is proper.

The serenades continue. Would you deprive me of that Spanish amusement? Good heavens, how severe you are!

There are an infinity of things that keep me at Naples; I will write you all about them. There is nothing in them, but they help to pass away the time.

Good-by. Scold me oftener; that does me an immense amount of good.

Devotedly yours.

To her Aunt.

FLORENCE.

Dear Aunt:

Do me the favor to manage so that we may remain some time longer in Florence, which is the most beautiful city in the world. Bring the money yourself, I beg of you; be amiable.

Have they not yet sent anything from Paris? Write or telegraph; it is better to telegraph. I cannot remain without gowns, especially here, and my dresses are all old. I do not look like myself. Telegraph to Worth, to Laferrière, to Reboux, to Ferry, to Vertus. Simply tell them to send me what I have ordered, that is all. There will be a ball here, perhaps,—and you cannot imagine how anxious I am to look well. Do not be uneasy about my face; it will be beautiful. My complexion is fresh; ask mamma if she does not think so. For a week past I have been going to bed early and I shall continue to do so. But it is atrocious to be in want of gowns, especially at Florence, where they dress so elegantly.

There is no comparison between this place and Naples. And then, when I am not dressed according to my taste, I am out of temper, and when I am out of temper I am ugly.

Love to you and papa. Good-by.

P. S.—Do not give rein to your imagination; X—— is not at Florence, and it is not he that is in question.

To the Marquis of C——.

June 26.

We had indeed already heard the dreadful news, Marquis, but, announced by you, the impression produced upon us was doubly painful. We are profoundly touched by your thinking of us at such a time.

I do not wish to weary you by conventional expressions of condolence, but I want you to be persuaded that your grief has found an echo in our hearts. I should like, too, to say to your mother, who is so good and so sympathetic, that in her great affliction God has granted her a supreme blessing in the excellent son whom we know and who so well deserves such a mother.

I should like to give expression to all the words of sympathy that crowd from my heart to my lips, but consoling words do not console. We hope, dear Marquis, to see you next year, if not gay, as formerly, at least recovered from your grief.

Good-by, and God keep you.

THE HORATII TAKING THE OATH OF THE "GRUTLI," OR RECONCILIATION, WHICH IT WILL BE YOUR PART TO BRING ABOUT.

To M——.[1]

And why is there a coolness between the two friends you mention? I had supposed that the cord which unites them in my picture was firmly tied (!).

My treatment at Enghien, where I go every morning at eight o'clock to remain until one in the afternoon, tires me excessively. And then, I detest Paris! It is a bazaar, a café, a gambling house, where one can only breathe, after one has been settled for a month in a house between a court and a garden. If you keep your windows closed you suffocate; if you open them you are deafened by the noise of the vehicles.

[1] An allusion to a sketch of Marie Bashkirtseff's, representing the two friends bound together by a cord fastened at its extremities around the neck of each, and having a heart hanging from its center.

My poor mandolin gives forth only plaintive sounds; but then all stringed instruments awaken innumerable sad recollections.

So, then, that good M—— says nothing bad about me? See what an excellent young man!

Well, I shall be more just to him for the future.

As for the place you will occupy in the other world, your natural goodness would take you to Heaven, but your dealings with the damned will relegate you

Intra color che son sospesi.

Ah! Monsieur, so you take an interest in Euterpe? That does not surprise me in so distinguished a man.

Since you asked me to do so, I will

willingly give you the heart-rending details of M——'s visit, and the consequences to which it led—for *Her*. Your friend, then, was as much of an *Œil de Bœuf*, of a *Talon Rouge*, as ever, and was followed, as usual, by his lackey, like Milord followed by his servant. It was a wise precaution to take. I pointed him out to the young person, who uttered a loud cry and ran away as fast as her legs could carry her, so that not one of the velocipedes which I dispatched in her pursuit was able to overtake her, and I have never since been able to find out what has become of her.

Instead of being moved by this disaster your friend continues to go to Monaco, sometimes with the ladies of our party, but always with his friend

F——, and followed by a page. Afterward Milord-and-his-servant breakfasted with us, but being on the eve of our departure we had nothing to set against his imposing train but a house in confusion, for which I shall never be able to console myself.

I must not forget to shower blessings upon you, according to my promise, in returning you the picture, a little injured, it is true, by the ravages of time.

As for the question in regard to which you promise me so touching a discretion, I will only ask you—do you by chance take me for the young harpist?

We shall remain ten days longer in Paris, waiting for the people from Nice, after which I do not know what we shall do until September, when we shall, perhaps, go to Biarritz; they say there will be a great many fashionable people there.

Do you still tame horses? Believe me, they are better than men. When a horse kicks you, you at least have the satisfaction of knowing that you have not been kicked by an ass.

Good-by. Ah, I was near forgetting to tell you that I think your letters charming, and to beg you not to neglect to write to me—under any pretense.

To M. de M——.

Schlangenbad, Badehaus.

This photograph is so pretty that I cannot resist the desire of letting you see to what a charming person you have been wanting in amiability. And

I, who had assigned you a place in the Inferno among the *Sospesi*, with Virgil and all those who, notwithstanding their virtues, cannot be admitted into Paradise, yet who, on the other hand, cannot be sent to hell, and are, consequently, suspended between the two! You deserve to be beside Lucifer himself at the very bottom of the pit.

Would you be displeased to be one of the *trinity?*[1] You would not, is it not so!

P. S.—If any of your friends are suffering from the nerves, send them here; mamma finds great relief from the waters of Schlangenbad.

[1] An allusion to the illustration which faces the preceding letter (see page 88).

To the Same.

PARIS, GRAND HOTEL.

Monsieur:

I had a mind not to write to you again, O Monsieur de M——, but I must always be writing something—no matter what—to some one. Women are often tiresome correspondents; if they are amiable they bore you to death with parodies of Madame de Sévigné; if they are ill-natured you must pay strict attention to what you say or else run the risk of being torn to pieces, Heaven knows by what sort of teeth— filled, broken, false—only to think of it makes me ill.

I see no one left to write to, then, but you, who are my friend and brother. Therefore, I accept your offer with gratitude.

Do you know that I, too, was to have gone to England to see my friend, Lady P——, but the poor woman has just died, and we shall doubtless not take the journey now.

We have just returned from Wiesbaden, where we spent some days after our return from pretty Schlangenbad, and where we met some very agreeable Russians—many old friends and some new acquaintances. Countess Loris Melikoff is staying there while her husband is playing the soldier in Asia.

My grandfather met there his old friend Prince Repnine, and after that he did not want to leave the place. In short, it was delightful, delightful; but alas, Monsieur, there were too many women!

We are here, awaiting a decision

of one kind or another. My throat is almost well, but I have been ordered to a warm climate. I do not know what we are going to do, and I hate myself. This is a very disagreeable feeling; one is like the thin woman taking a sea bath; it is no use for her to run, her legs go with her.

I have an excursion to propose to you to a much more agreeable place than that wretched Sorrento. And pray believe that I am in earnest. The project is to walk from Nice to Rome, stopping at all the interesting places on the way. We could make the journey in twenty-four days without excessive fatigue. The elder people would drive, I would go on foot, all in one party. I am waiting for letters from England. What do you say to that?

In any case we shall see each other in Italy, and I count upon receiving from you a clap on the shoulder, which will be energetically given, to judge from your exhibitions of strength at Naples; so that the sole idea of shaking hands with you and taking you to present your respects to mamma makes me cry out.

Well I will do all I can, as friendship commands.

Regards from all.

To Mlle. Colignon.

SUNDAY, October 14.

Ah, dear friend, how is it possible not to adore Verdi! I know nothing more wonderful than his "Aïda." Each chord, each phrase speaks. I truly think one could understand the whole story and know in what country the action was taking place without seeing the scenery or hearing the words. It is in this sense that I place "Aïda" above all the other music I know. And what melody, what force, what delicacy of sentiment!

You know that I do not speak from a scientific point of view. I could not do so, and it would be so much the worse if I could. One is more—one enjoys a work more thoroughly when one does not know how it is composed.

As I do not intend to devote myself seriously to music, I have learned only so much of it as a person of taste who does not intend to compose should know.

It was this evening, as I was playing some airs from "Aïda" on my mandolin, that I first realized how beautiful the opera is. I had forgotten the music. Music disposes to life, to gayety, to tears, to love, in short to whatever agitates, pleases, or torments, while drawing is an occupation which raises one above earthly things and renders one indifferent to everything but one's art.

They made me take a drive in the Bois; the weather was delightful and the air so balmy that I fancied myself in Italy. It will be necessary to give notice for Sunday.

It vexes me to lose a day every week in this way; it bores me to be doing nothing.

No doubt the study of music requires as much application, as much patience, but, however little one plays, whether one plays to please one's self or for others, one must have a genuine feeling for it.

However devoted one may be to drawing or painting, they would never cause one——

It makes me wild to be unable to express my thoughts!

And then what I have to say is very trite. All I wish is to make known what my own views on these matters are.

The music of "Aïda" is like that of the "Gretchen" of Max. That speaks, that tells you the whole story even to its slightest details. So that one could tell, merely by hearing the music, whether the scene was laid in a room or out of doors, whether the time was day or night.

While I am discoursing about these abstruse matters, "France awaits breathlessly" the result of the elections. For they take place to-day. The marshal must have dined with a bad appetite last night. I regret so much to have no one to keep me *au courant* of all these machinations.

1878.

To M. de M——.

PARIS, 67 AVENUE DE L'ALMA.

I hasten, dear Monsieur, to dispel your natural anxiety; the cakes have arrived; they are superb and we thank you for them; they are so beautiful that one feels tempted to have them put in a frame.

We have met with a great misfortune; our dear doctor, Wolitski, whom you have seen at our house, died last Saturday at two o'clock in the morning. He was one of our best friends and grandpapa's godson, and we have all grown up under his eyes. You may well imagine that such a loss is irreparable. Friends like him are rare indeed. Grandpapa, ill himself, as you know, cried all day and is still very sad. But I will not dwell longer on so gloomy a subject.

You ask me which I prefer—art or the beautiful in nature; I prefer neither; I admire both equally, but the beautiful in nature gives complete delight only when one is conscious of artistic power—which is a great, a very great power.

There is a person here who wishes to know everything bad that is said about a certain M. L——. Do you know him?

You know Princess S—— has sailed for America, where, they say, she intends to marry. That would be indeed an extraordinary termination.

How happy you must be at the

thought of going to Rome! I confess that I envy you, although envy is a base passion.

Tell me all about the king's funeral, and about everything else beside. Be good and write me all the news—and all the old things you can think of. I shall read your letter while I eat, for it is only then that I am free.

They send you a thousand kind regards. Are we to have a carnival?

To the Same.

My white dog Pincio, which you have seen at our house, has just been stolen. I think they have taken him out of Paris. I am writing in all directions, in the hope that some one of the charitable souls to whom I address myself may catch the wretches who have taken him.

Can you imagine anything more base than to steal a dog? Such an action is simply vile. What! To take from its home a creature which is attached to its master, which is more intelligent than many bipeds, but which is unable to defend itself—this is the acme of meanness and wickedness.

You are happy. You have no dog to be stolen from you. Well, patience!

What is to be done? I have advertised in the papers, offering a reward of two hundred francs for his recovery, but without result. Are not such people a disgrace to humanity?

Console me by speaking to me of Italy,

To Mlle. B——.

How good and amiable you are, my dear Jeanne, to think of me in these moments when one forgets everything!

Mamma and I are enchanted at your happiness, for I take it for granted that you are happy.

Is it possible you have been in Nice? I knew nothing of it; no one told me anything. But tell me, how did you find our house, since you did not know our address?

I spent the winter in Rome, where I studied painting.

When I see you again, I will paint your portrait. Give me news of all your family, and send me, without fail, the likeness of your *fiancé*. I must see the happy man who has won for his wife Jeanne, who, both in mind and heart, is a treasure. Show him these words, and tell him they were written by one who never flatters and who never exaggerates.

This winter, in Rome, I was asked in marriage by an Englishman and by two Italian counts. But I refused them all. They loved me, but I did not love them; that was all. Besides, I did not wish to marry so young; I am scarcely seventeen. How old are you?

You ask my address. Direct my letters to " Mlle. Marie Bashkirtseff, at her villa at Nice, 55 *bis*, Promenade des Anglais." My aunt has given me this villa. They will forward me my letters from Nice if I am elsewhere. That is the safest way.

Answer quickly, and tell me where and when you are to be married, and the name of your future husband, and send me his photograph.

I have been back in Nice for a fortnight; the city is deserted, and I take refuge in my books. Perhaps you do not know how serious and studious I am by nature, wild and gay as I can be when there is any cause for merriment.

When and where shall I see you?

It is so good of you not to have forgotten me. Rest assured that if anything particular should happen, I will tell you of it without delay.

Good-by; a thousand kind regards to your family from all of us. I embrace you with my whole heart, and I wish you every kind of happiness, possible and impossible.

To the Same.

Paris, Avenue de l'Alma.

Dear Jeanne:

I have not been able to answer your letter until to-day, for it was not until to-day that we met our relatives, who gave us your address. I have thought of you very often, I wished so much to write to you after receiving the news of your marriage.

I am able to do so only a year after that event. I hope you will not think my silence was owing to indifference or forgetfulness.

I hear great news about you. Write to me soon; I shall not lose your address again, and I will be able to answer you.

We are almost settled at Paris. I

spend my time painting and go very little into society which, indeed, bores me greatly. We all send you our love and hope you will continue to be as happy as you have been up to the present.

Good-by, dear; I send you my likeness in case you should have forgotten the face of Marie Bashkirtseff.

To her Mother.

SODEN, August 1.

Dear Mamma:

First, pray give me news of grandpapa's health;[1] next, Soden, by dint of being dull, has become amusing. I will tell you all about it. One of the

[1] Her grandfather had received a stroke of paralysis.

most *chic* families of St. Petersburg arrived here at the same time as old Prince Ouroussoff, whose sister, who is married to M. Maltzoff, is the intimate friend of our Empress, as you know. The Russian ladies of our circle imagine that the indifference of the two little German princes, whom I have already mentioned to you, mortifies me. "That spoiled child," said Madame A——, "who is accustomed to see her slightest caprice obeyed, is mortified by the coldness—only apparent evidently—of these gentlemen."

For my part such a thing had never even occurred to me, dear mamma. I am only amused to see how prone people are, both at Soden and elsewhere, to credit one with sentiments, opinions, and thoughts which one has never entertained. For a couple of days, indeed, my thoughts wandered occasionally to the little princes, but at the end of that time, I had ceased to think about them. But since people have spoken of the matter, I will confess to you that I have never even taken a good look at them. However, I can inform you that the younger (eighteen), Hans, is tall, blonde, has a large, rather delicate nose, small eyes, a shrewd mouth, wears no mustache, walks headlong, and has the expression of a young wolf.

The other, August (twenty-four or twenty-five), who is smaller, is dark, has very fine eyes, a slight black drooping mustache—indeed in his whole person there is something of a droop— a velvety skin, such as I do not think I have ever before seen in a man; a handsome mouth, a regular nose, neither round nor pointed, nor aquiline nor classic—a nose of which, too, the skin is delicate, a thing which is exceedingly rare; and a very pale complexion, which would be beautiful, if it were not the result of ill health. Both princes have handsome hands—aristocratic and well-cared for.

How, then, would I describe them if I looked well at them!

Write to me every day, and tell me all about grandpapa.

Aunt joins me in love to all.

To the Same.

SODEN, Saturday, August 3.

Have I mentioned M. Muhle, the landlord, to you? Well, M. Muhle pretends that it was got up on our account. You know there was a ball at the Kurhaus to-night, and this poor Muhle, who is always drunk, promised himself that the entertainment would prove a brilliant success. Of course we all went.

We had scarcely taken our places when I caught sight of a gentleman whom I had already seen once or twice of a morning, driving an odd-looking tilbury, with a little groom. Well, this gentleman came and joined us. He is the Baron—I have forgotten what—son of I don't know what official of the place, a grand seignior, according to what I am told. But I refused to dance, and, as he insisted, I tried to prove to him that dancing is undignified, that that exercise is one of the most convincing proofs of the decadence of the great human family. Finally, I talked politics to him, spoke of the war in the East, etc., etc. Muhle was vexed, because by refusing to dance with this pink and white young man, I offended the young man, who immediately left Soden.

Every one joked so much about the Prince of H—— that it makes me laugh now to think of it. This poor prince deteriorates visibly. When he came here he was handsome, and now he is ugly and ill-tempered. We can all recognize his ring, and you should hear how he speaks to the waiter and to his poor brother. I think they will soon bury him. What a horrible malady!

The Baron—he of the ball—is the chief functionary of the country, governor or something of the kind, I do not know just what. Prince Ouroussoff is acquainted with the said baron, who never ceases to tell him that to occupy the position he does, young as he is, is an honor which he does not deserve; that he does not think he owes it at all to his own merits, but solely to the emperor's goodness. But this is only the beginning. The baron *is in love with a young lady*, and in order to make her acquaintance, he got up last night's ball. But as they told him here that another young man was in love with the girl, he went in quest of this young man, and, with the frankness befitting the occasion, begged him to tell him the truth, and if there was no foundation for the report, and he did not love the young lady, to give him his permission to seek an introduction to her; but if, on the contrary, the report was true, to acknowledge it to be so, in which case his sense of justice and his integrity would prevent him from interfering to imperil the other's chances of success, he having the right of priority. The gentleman assured him that he was not at all in love with the girl (poor girl), and consented to his visiting her as much as he chose.

The young girl—was I; the gentleman—D——.

The baron is tall, fair, stout, florid. You know that kind of men generally admire me and that I as generally detest them. It is true, indeed, that when I look into my heart, I find I do not care much more for any of the others. Count M——— was fair; Count B———, fair; Pacha G——— (what a name!), fair; P———, fair; Count M———, fair, and finally Baron S———, fair. A———, who was only a boy, was also fair.

I miss you all very much and my studio still more.

Good-by; kiss grandpapa for me.

To the Same.

SODEN, August 6.

Dear Mamma:

I am going to tell you about my childish doings. This morning I went out to take a walk and entered a Catholic church. I availed myself of the absolute solitude of the place to go up into the pulpit, to go into the choir, to go on the altar, and to read the prayers placed on the tablets of the altar; I did all this by way of prayer, for I have a multitude of projects in which I need the assistance of Heaven. But the thought that I have read a mass transports me. Only think, I rang the bell as the priests do during mass! At all events, my intentions were not bad.

I have had a long conversation with Prince Ouroussoff. As we were talking the prince suddenly said to me, "There are the Ganzes." You remember that I gave the name "Ganz" to the two German princes. You can imagine that I could not remain serious when this dignified person, this statesman, stopped in the middle of an explanation of the secret causes of the war to utter so simple a phrase as, "There are the Ganzes." The word "Ganzes" made me think of the German *gans*.[1]

I made a sketch of the princes (as I did at Nice), so like them that the waiter, who was passing with a tray, stopped short before the canvas and began to laugh and gesticulate in such a way that my vanity as an artist was indeed flattered.

Then Madame A—— came. We stood at the window, which is our balcony. Ganz passed and repassed to look at us. Madame A—— played the coquette, laughing in a way that was in very bad taste. How stupid it is

[1] A goose.

that I cannot make you share my amusement on the subject of the Ganzes.

Good-by. With love.

1879.

To M——.

Paris, 63 Avenue de l'Alma.

Your letter has this one good result for you—that it irresistibly provokes advice which I find it impossible to refrain from giving you, even though it has not been asked:

1st. Never speak of rights which have been *granted* you, or of favors which *have not been refused* to you, to speak more exactly.

2d. Never return a guitar in bad condition.

3d. Never wait until you are insulted, if you really wish to fight.

And finally, be a good Christian and write without the hope of having your letters read or answered, or that they will not be made public.

To Mlle. Colignon.

MAY.

My Dear Friend:

I ought to tell you that having finished painting at four o'clock I have spent the time since then in reading "The Nabob," a novel of Alphonse Daudet. It is very interesting, and this sort of nabob would resemble one of another sort if he were refined and ennobled. I know that the comparison is not a flattering one, and it is for this reason I say that he must be refined, ennobled, spiritualized. That is, I am not quite certain, I distrust my own judgment; when one is romantic, I think one is apt to take affectation for distinction, and when any one seems to me strong and out of the common, I fear that he may be only rustic, vulgar, *bourgeois*. Happy, happy he who knows how to express his thoughts! I write to you as if I were writing in my journal. No, not that; if I were to trouble myself as to the way in which I should express in my journal all the fancies that come into my head it would be indeed too ridiculous.

Well, then, listen. As to fancies, look at the simple-minded Joyeuse in the Nabob; you have no doubt observed that in the matter of imagination he resembles me exactly; I, too, can weave out of a word a novel, ten novels, twenty novels, and all in a second's time. Some of them, however, last for weeks. No, there are moments of lassitude when one would like to end everything; and to end everything there are only two ways—to die or to fall in love.

Ah, if you knew how weary I am of this life of sadness, in which everything crosses us, everything evades us, everything mocks us!

Devotedly yours.

To her Brother.

PARIS, November.

Dear Paul:

M. Gavini sent us two tickets to-day, and we went to the new Chamber. I like Versailles better. One meets more people whom one knows when all are obliged to leave by the same train. Here every one goes away when he chooses, and there is not the amusing sight of the people all going out together, as in the other. The visitors are more fashionable than at Versailles, but the boxes are a little like those at the theater—all alike; and the President's box, in which we were, differs in no way from the others.

Every one was in his usual place. C—— looked bent and languid; Gambetta seemed to me thin; Bescherelle ran about as usual. I examined the magnificent Gobelins and the frightful statuary.

Rouher made his appearance in the Chamber—the Chamber at Paris, the old legislative body—for the first time to-day since the death of the unfortunate prince. He must have had strange visions.

It pains me to think how this man must have suffered since the prince's death; he must be very unhappy. G—— told me he was vexed with him for not pointing out to him the box in which I was.

Yesterday we dined with M. M——. I complimented Gaillard on his *Chant des races latines,* published in Madame Adam's *Review.* He is a young man from Avignon, with irregular features and a Saracenic cast of countenance, and a lock of hair standing up on his head that, with his pompousness and exaggerated Southern languor, gave him an absurd air. I chatted with him and he proposed to me to do something for the

Review—to translate for it from the Russian.

You may imagine that I was delighted, and that I will do it whenever he wishes.

Ah! I forgot to tell you that this morning mamma had a great success at the Russian church. The Grand Duke Nicholas saluted her and spoke to her. The Grand Duke asked her if any member of her family was decorated with the order of Saint George. (The occasion of the mass was the fête of the Chevaliers of Saint George.) Mamma answered that during the war of the Crimea, in the storming of the Malakoff, her brother, at the time hardly sixteen, was decorated by him on the field of battle. The Grand Duke recalled the fact and was extremely gracious, saying that heroism was a family trait, since she had not been afraid to leave the house with such frightful weather.

Good-by. With love.

To M. X——.

You ask me, my friend, how I received the great news.

I received it with murmuring. Having put myself outside all that constitutes the life of women, I can speak from the height on which I stand without that feeling of delicacy which prevents one from expressing one's mind freely in things where one's self is concerned.

What has happened to you, then? Are you in the case of the singer who retires from the stage while people can still say, What a pity! This idea pleases me; if you have taken the step, however, without this powerful reason, I should see that I was mistaken in you. I took you for a public monument, a possession of the nation. Imagine yourself the Arc de Triomphe or the Louvre passed into the hands of a private individual. I would forgive you for it only in the case that I were the person favored, just as I should think it monstrous if those monuments were given to any one but me—which would be equally extraordinary, but excusable in my eyes. You deceive yourself, my friend; remember your past. I know very well that you are saying to yourself, "In my case it is different"—as every one does who takes the same step.

I shall have no more consideration for you, certain as I am that nothing can turn you from the new path, that is to say, the same old path—the same piece of music, only that this time you will play the base, you will be the accompaniment—to the ball, to the play. But these warnings are in vain; nothing in the world could prevent the event; a man who has inspired so many passions, broken so many hearts, been false to so many vows, must of necessity marry. It is an expiation.

To her Brother.

Paris, Wednesday, December 10.
Dear Paul:

We have been to the Dominican Convent to see Father Didon.

Need I tell you that Father Didon is the preacher who for the last two years has been rising so rapidly into fame and of whom all Paris is just now talking? He had expected us. As soon as we arrived they sent to notify him and we waited in a little reception room with glazed walls and floor, furnished with a table, three chairs, and a small stove. I saw his portrait yesterday and I already knew that he had fine eyes (a beauty which L—— P—— does not possess). He entered looking very amiable, very much like a man of the world, and very handsome in his beautiful white woolen robe, which reminded me of the gowns I wear in the house. But for his tonsure his head would resemble P. de C.'s. He looks brighter, however, his eyes have a franker look, and his attitude is more natural, though extremely dignified. His features begin to grow heavy and his mouth has the same disagreeably crooked look that C.'s has. But he is very distinguished-looking, without any of the exaggerated charm of the creole; he carries his head erect; he has a pale complexion, a fine forehead, beautiful white hands; a gay, and even, as far as possible, a jovial air. One would like to see him with a mustache. Notwithstanding his dignified manner, he is very witty. One can see plainly that he is fully aware of his popularity, that he is accustomed to adoration, and that he is sincerely delighted with the sensation he creates everywhere!

Mother M—— had naturally written to him, telling him what a wonder he was going to see, and I spoke to him about painting his portrait.

He did not refuse, although he said it would be difficult, almost impossible— a young girl painting the portrait of Father Didon—he is so much before the public—so much talked about.

But it is precisely for that reason, idiot!

I was presented to him as a fervent admirer of his. I had never either seen him or heard him speak before, but I imagined him just as he was, with the same inflections of voice, at times low and persuasive, at times so loud as to be almost startling, even when conversing on ordinary subjects.

This is a portrait that I feel thoroughly capable of executing, and if it could be arranged I should esteem myself very fortunate.

This devil of a monk cannot be very good, I think. Even before seeing him I was a little afraid of him. That would be disagreeable—a monk! A person who might acquire an influence over me, and that is a thing I do not at all desire.

He promised to come and see us, and for a moment I had the hope he would keep his promise.

But that was foolish, and all that I desire now is that he should consent to sit for me.

Nothing in the world would better serve to further my ambition as an artist.

With love.

1880.

To A—— M——.

34 Avenue Montaigne,
Paris, Saturday, July 3.

I have hesitated long before sending this. You yourself have so well understood that I could not write to you that you have disguised, even to yourself, the request that I should do so under an appeal to my good feelings in general—a delicacy of sentiment unconscious on your part, but for which I am obliged to you.

If the question were simply to answer the letter of a young man who is in love, I should not answer it.

So then, let us understand each other well. *This is not a letter.* I do not know whether I flatter you or not in supposing you capable of grasping the distinction. You are young, and you seem to be the victim of a genuine passion. (We shall see later whether this is the case or not.) That goes a great way. It would please me to improve a fellow-being, by exercising over him whatever good influence I might possess. This would be a serious and an interesting undertaking; a noble task, which I should always be willing to undertake. This, then, is what makes me write; this, and an irresistible inclination to laugh a little at your stratagems; this is an easy triumph, however.

Listen, then—the want of candor, whether in important matters or in trifles, is equally repugnant to me.

What also inspires me with a doubt as to the genuineness of the feeling you profess to entertain for me is that this feeling, had it been genuine, would have opened up to you a superior world, as it were, and would have endowed you, for the time, at least, with faculties which would make you comprehend that with natures like mine a man would find favor only by laying aside all artifice,—but do not try this,—by laying bare his heart and his life as he would before God.

And you—what do you do?

Do you think, then, that real facts, however insignificant they might be, would amuse me less than your little inventions—even though they should be interesting to me only as human documents! And you still speak of confiding your sorrows to me as if I had forbidden you to do so. You quote the Manual which you do not understand.

You are only a child.

The moment in which I showed you so much kindness as to give you the choice between an immediate dismissal and a delay of six months, you should have paid me the compliment of taking me for your patron and counselor. That is a rôle which one never refuses, however proud one may be.

You might even have kept me informed of your doings, in order to spare my mind the fatigue of seeking to discover the truth, in case I should care to discover it.

Here is a great deal of talk, you will say, about silly trifles, like the telegraphic dispatches which required your *immediate* presence ; and that *later* letter (which you had the time to wait for), where I do not know, and which made it unnecessary for you to go away—innocent anachronism.

I grant that there was no imperative reason to make you go away, and that, while your heart had some part in the matter, it was right that you should think, too, of its practical side. This was quite natural. But why disguise this prose, honest enough in itself, under the pretense of a great passion. This was a want of consideration for yourself. For it was certainly remarkable that events should have all coincided so that you should be there just in time to receive your relatives' commission.

How simple you are! A lie when it is not managed with adroitness attracts the attention like a glaring color, and a useless lie is as disgusting as a base action.

Why say, for instance, that X——'s apartment is immense? I know it is only a moderate-sized room. This trifle proves to you that there are no trifles. It is sufficient to analyze a single drop of water to know what are the properties of the whole spring.

I shall not destroy your letter.

If you wish that I should undertake your improvement, I must have documents, in order to know whether I have succeeded or not. If you are a good pupil you will make a true friend of me, and if you understand my character you know that my friendship will be sincere.

But are you worthy of all this? And if things do not turn out according to your wishes, will you not foolishly bear me ill will for having loved me?

You have written nonsense, as you say, but begin over again. The question now is your morality, not at all your worldly projects. I consider you audacious to have aspired to my hand, but does not the proverb say that the soldier who does not aspire to become one day a marshal of France is a bad soldier?

I am conscious, finally, that what I ask from you is impossible. It would exact a complete change of character.

They say, though I do not think so,

that love works miracles. In short, the easy fashion in which you have accepted this separation has affected me disagreeably.

If you do not *feel* the truth of my sermons, I shall give up preaching them; and as for you, go in peace.

Whenever you grow impatient or, like a commonplace person, fancy your rôle a ridiculous one, consult the little *Manual of the Perfect Lover;* it will give you the measure of your feelings.

Let us assume as a fixed principle that there is no baseness in the person loved to which one does not try to give a favorable explanation; that there is nothing in the world which one would not do for the beloved person with real satisfaction; no so-called *sacrifice* which one would not make with joy. For love, after all, is a selfish sentiment, and the proof of this is that one is happier in loving than in being loved. But all this is neither required nor commanded; the lover performs it naturally because he experiences a personal satisfaction in doing so. When there is the least hesitation, the least impatience; one should not, one cannot think that one loves. You will see, then, whether or not you will bear these few months of trial,—*at the end of which there will be, after all, only an uncertainty*,—not with patience only, but with pleasure.

All this, *ad libitum*.

AMEN.

To M. Julian.

Noumea, Mont Dore,
July, August.

Yes, citizen director, everything is here, even to the special costume one is compelled to wear, like the galley-slaves; and attired in this costume it is that we undergo the rough treatment of the baths from five to seven every morning. The doctor at the springs assures me that it is beneficial, but the people connected with these places are all alike; all they want is to get possession of one. It is a very great pity that T—— does not come. You I do not invite. Paris has need of you. But how much good a short exile here would do you!

Just fancy, there is nothing to eat.

It is unworthy of an exalted soul to think of food; but alas! if it were not that I fear to become anæmic— The doctor tried to make me believe that I was so already. "Do you feel very weak, Mademoiselle?" he asked. "By no means, Monsieur," I answered. "Are you habitually pale?" "On the contrary." "Easily fatigued?" "Not at all." "That makes no difference; you are very weak." "But how do you make that out, Monsieur?" I asked. "It is impossible to explain, but such is the case."

So that, if I were not afraid of losing strength, I should eat even less than I do, so repugnant is the food. Ah! succulent dishes of Lake St. Fargeau! You gave me a foretaste, as it were, of the products of the Trompette of Mont

Doré. But how much better you were!

I must not neglect to acknowledge the justice of your criticisms on my drawing.

My aunt sends you her best remembrances. It is not to my family that you owe this epistle, illustrious before its author has become so (to copy Rochefort); you owe it to the fact that I want to put you in a good humor.

Who would tighten the screw at a critical moment? What you say about the fifty artisans—this employing so many hands on the same piece of work—is it not one of those maneuvers to brutalize the people, made use of under the rule of the ever-to-be-execrated Cæsars, to extinguish the intelligence of the working-classes? You make use, too, of the words *lead to*—words to be regarded with suspicion since they were pronounced by the illustrious humbug who still conceals his sentiments under republican flowers of oratory.

For a moment I thought you had atoned for all those things which it pains me to have to reproach a good patriot with; yes, for a moment I took this marriage of the two silhouettes for the greatly-to-be-desired alliance with the country of the Inquisition, and I was rejoiced at it. All the Latin peoples are brothers, and it would please me to see France extirpating the last vestige of—in the country in question. I deceived myself.

Leave me room for hope. Then,

whatever be our differences, let us be true to the Republic,—Athenian, Spartan, federal, socialistic, orthopædic, artistic, medalistic, Tonyfic, and even Rodolphiphobic.

Long live the Republic!

To her Brother.

PARIS, 1880.

Dear Paul:

I am going to tell you about a proposal I have received from a prince; he dined with us, and during the evening he whispered in my ear that he wished to speak to me. My aunt was chatting with C——, and I consented to hear what he had to say.

"Ought I to marry?" he began.

Do you see the trick, dear Paul?

"Yes, if you wish to do so," I answered.

"I do not wish to do so."

"Then do not marry. Is that all you had to say to me?"

"No; I once told you that I loved you; well, I love you still. You will understand that it is a torture for me to come here in the circumstances. I am sick of it."

"And why are you sick of it? I thought you liked it."

"I do, but whenever I say anything to you, you insult me."

"Not at all; I am gay, and if I adorn our conversations with digressions, it is because, as you know, you leave an eternal time between your sentences."

"You will not laugh at me?"

"No, no, indeed; I am very serious."

But instead of answering, he looked at me, and I saw that his eyes had dark circles under them, and that his forehead was even paler than usual.

"I must go away, must I not," he said at last, "and come here no more?"

"Why so?"

"Because I love you."

We had to speak in low tones in order not to be heard by the others, and this lent a sort of tender charm to our voices.

"I have told you that I love you, and when one loves a young girl there are not twenty ways of settling the question, are there? It can end only in one way or the other. Well, then I must return no more."

"And why?" (I played the innocent).

"Because I suffer too much in coming."

Then his eyes filled with tears. There was something childlike and winning in this emotion, but the handkerchief with which he wiped his eyes spoiled everything.

"Oh, come, come," I said, but without laughing, "tears are all very well, but they should not be wiped away by a bit of linen, but by—her who has caused them to flow."

He made an impatient movement.

"Everything is not rose-colored in this world," I resumed seriously; "not by any means rose-colored. My system of doing what gives one pleasure— is good, but it is not practicable; one can avoid doing what pains one, but as for doing what pleases one——"

"Listen to me, Mademoiselle, and do not insult me; do not laugh at me. Either I shall go away forever, or you must authorize me to return; things cannot continue as they are now, I am too unhappy, I suffer too much; I am ill. When a man loves a girl he must either marry her or part from her forever."

"Listen," I returned, "it is easy to say, marry her, but to do so—that depends——"

"On whom?"

"Why, on her, of course."

"Well, then?"

(He is young and he must have felt a little emotion, even if he remembered my dowry.)

"Well, then, for my part, I do not wish to engage myself; and then I don't know that it is necessary to wait. How do I know what you are? You seem to be an honest man, but perhaps you are not one. Marriage lasts a long time, a very long time. I do not believe in your love, which, however, may be sincere. I should like to be certain that it is so. So, you see, we must wait."

"How long?"

"Let us see (I began to count on my fingers), "five, six,—until New Year's day."

"That is too long."

"Well, then, until Christmas, let us say Christmas; seven months."

"And if, at the end of that time you are convinced of my

love, Mademoiselle, you will consent?"

"Ah, no, I do not say that, Monsieur; that would be to engage myself; I do not wish to engage myself. I do not love you, but this delay is necessary to enlighten us with regard to our mutual feelings."

"And then you will need three months more to come to a decision?"

"Oh, no, I will tell you my decision immediately."

And then I played the child, the innocent. After being by turns pensive, serious, and sarcastic, I spoke of my painting. "How could I possibly marry? I must paint. And then, might I not die?"

"I will paint with you, Mademoiselle."

"Just so; and in these seven months you will learn to draw."

And then I began to praise a student's life; I spoke to him of my dowry, saying that that had a good deal to do with his love. Naturally, he pretended to be indignant.

"Do you suppose that I could not find money if I wished! Do I even know how much you have? I scorn your fortune. It is yourself I love."

Well, dear Paul, I do not love him. I have not even that vague sentiment for him which I had for X——.

"In fixing this delay of seven months, do you leave me room for hope?"

"You should always hope, even if I were to give you a decisive no. Besides, I have found—I want you to copy something for me which I will afterward correct. Here is the document." He agreed.

In short, I exact no promise from him; he says he loves me, and I give him the opportunity of finding out whether this is the case or not. That is all. It is amusing, is it not?

To-morrow I will write again.

Good-by.

To Princess K——.

What a bore it is, dear Princess, that you are not in Paris! Only think, Gambetta is going to give a splendid fête. We have an invitation, but mamma and my aunt do not wish to go on account of their mourning, and as I know no one among the Republicans I am in such despair at being obliged to give up this entertainment,—which will in truth be very amusing, and very odd, and very magnificent,—that I am tempted to go to Dieppe in quest of you. Indeed you should return to Paris, at least for that day. Dieppe is so near, only four hours, four times the distance to Versailles. It is only an excursion. If you wish, two of us will go to see you to try and persuade you. Think of it! the first entertainment at Leon's house. All the *élite* of the republican party will be there ; it will be a unique and, in a measure, a historic spectacle. Roasting an ox is nothing to the preparations they are making. What grieves me a little is that young A——

will not be there, owing to the stupidity of his grandfather, who has taken it into his head to fall ill. But I can easily console myself for his absence.

Come, consent; without you I shall be compelled to remain at home. I am acquainted only with Bonapartists who, if I were to tell them that I was going to the Presidential box, would look on me as a positively disgusting person.

Answer quickly.

With love.

1881.

To M. X——.

Monsieur:

I send you a plan,[1] with the north well marked.[2] Now I will give you my ideas in the matter, to serve you in some sort as a guide. The studio should be two stories high and should have three windows, besides a skylight. Below the studio another studio, for sculpture, on the ground floor.

You understand that there are to be no living apartments in that part of the building. I have also marked in pencil the divisions that have occurred to

[1] See plan, pages 163, 164.

[2] Reference is here made to a project entertained at the time by the Bashkirtseff family of building a house in Paris, on the Avenue Kleber. This project, however, was never realized.

me; you will see if they are practicable.

I should like the studio to communicate with the *salons*. On the ground floor, then, a studio for sculpture, kitchens, etc. First floor—*salons* and studios. Second floor—bedrooms, servants' rooms. I see that a bedroom and a dressing-room might be made for me on the first floor, and the studio still be large enough and my bedroom sixteen feet wide. Or, if you could manage to give the studio a regular form, that would be much better.

The only thing I am particular about is that the studio should follow the *salons;* and, to economize space, the coach-house could be put under the dining-room. You see that I have contrived to leave space for a garden in

1881.
34 avenue Montaigne

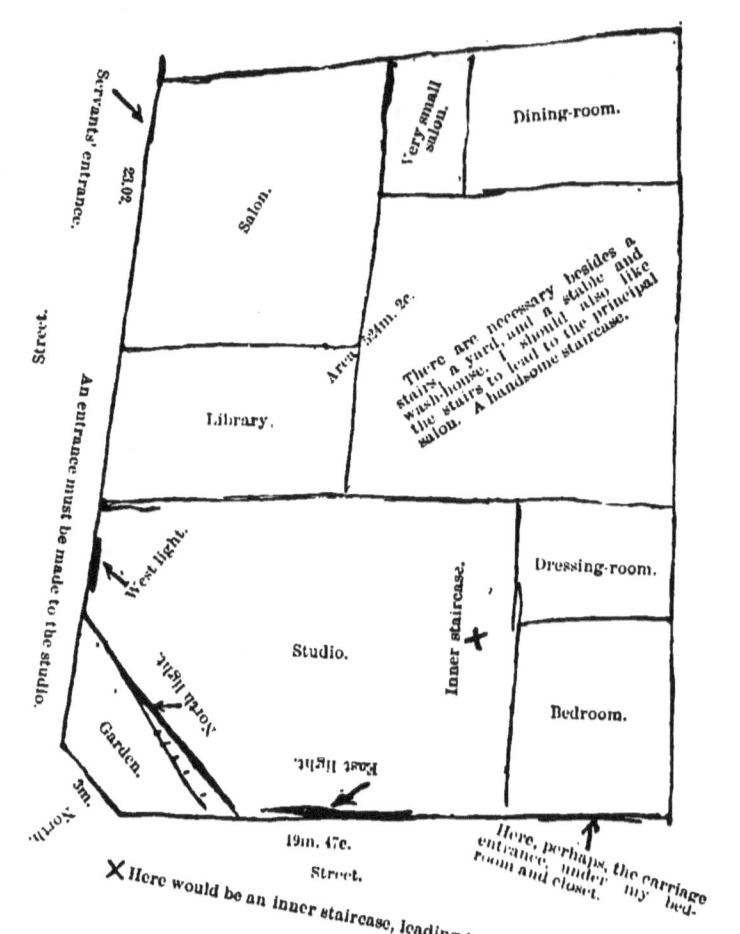

front of the studio by which this might be entered, as studios should have a separate entrance. If necessary, my bedroom and closet might be on the second floor, and I could enter the studio by the inner stairs.

But, above all, let the principal entrance be arranged so that it will be necessary to pass through the *salon* and the library before reaching the studio. Let the rooms follow one another, in short.

I hope you will be able to understand these incoherencies, and excuse the confusion of my architectural ideas.

Accept, Monsieur, my compliments.

P. S.—Perhaps it would be possible to locate the garden (even if it should only have an area of 50 meters) so that I could work there without being seen from the street. I do not insist upon the outside garden; in the place which I have marked for it there might be merely a little garden two yards deep.

All these, however, are only suggestions. But I think the garden would be well located where I have marked it on the plan.

There will be necessary, besides, a staircase, a yard, a stable, and a coach-house. I should like the staircase to lead to the principal *salon*.

To M. Julian.

Poltava, Russia,
May 21 (June 2).

White draperies, sorrowful eyes, pale hands, an apathetic air—the kingdom of this country is not for me! (subject of a sketch for the landscape.)

Oh! the horrible mastodons! people whose attitudes and hands are like those in poor old paintings. Can one help being angry, then? You are a great prophet, but those hundred hours in a railway-carriage were what I needed. So far, however, all I have gained by them is a cold. The air, delightfully pure and balmy, is too cold to remain long out of doors, and I keep inside. I have got myself into this, but it is none the less vexatious on that account. If, at least, it were the severe majesty of the steppes; but no, the country is pretty. The family are extremely attentive—the younger ones think me delightful, the older ones think I have grown serious and quiet.

Five years ago I came here to display my first long gowns, and I was as noisy and brilliant as an exhibition of fire-works; now I am in search of something between *forgetfulness* and *repose*. My head is full of painting and these people cannot understand the noble preoccupations of persons of our kind; and then it must be confessed that I am used up for the present.

Yesterday my father received a grand ovation, it being his fête-day. All the peasants assembled in the court-yard, cheered him, shook hands with him, embraced him; they made me take off my hat and veil to get a better look at me, and after they had looked at me it was my turn to be cheered and carried in triumph. I was obliged to embrace a number of them. Then the women came; I made my appearance on the balcony; fresh enthusiasm, one cry drowning all the others, "A good husband!" *Gambetta at Cahors, in short.*

Then when all this crowd had drunk and danced, they spoke of donations of lands, but some one let them see plainly it was of no use, and that ended this episode. They distribute among these good people, it appears, so-styled ukases of the Emperor, compelling the land-owners to give them dozens of things. A price has also been set on the heads of the nobles—50 rubles a head. Do you not fancy you see mine already at the end of a pike? In short, if you recall the history of the past years of your *ancien régime*, you will understand how things are here.

The resemblance between the two periods is striking—from the frightful condition of the people to the stupid blindness of the nobles. The French peasant sacking the château, saying that it grieves him to the heart to do so, but that the king commands it, is the brother of the Russian who pretends to have received orders to massacre the Jews.

Only think that I was not able to have an easel at Poltava. An amiable native went a journey of twelve hours by rail in search of one; which was at least obliging on his part. Here there is only a photograph painter and there is no means of obtaining a canvas sufficiently large for a picture. Ah, if you but knew!

How is M. Tony Robert-Fleury?

I left him ill. What if he should "shuffle off this mortal coil"? That would interfere horribly with my habits and then, joking apart, I like him greatly, and you also.

P. S.—Paul has grown stout; his wife is pretty, and everything goes on well. Dina dresses elegantly, and enjoys herself, and I am no longer affected by popular triumphs. This is serious.

To her Father.

AUGUST.

Dear Father:

After the article in the journal, Jugeni Cray, it is absolutely necessary for me to make that image. Will you then be good enough to do what may be required in the matter, as I do not know how to set about it. Besides, as you are an intelligent being, I have recourse to you to procure me exact information. For instance, for what part of the church[1] the image is intended, its size, form, etc. For I suppose that it ought to be adapted to the arrangement of the interior decorations, and no doubt the principal images have been already ordered from celebrated Russian artists. In short, try to obtain something of importance for me so that I may feel satisfaction in doing it well. I should be very glad if it were life-size—a Christ, for instance, with the features of the Em-

[1] A church built in memory of the Emperor Alexander II, at St. Petersburg, on the spot where the Emperor was killed.

peror; in fine, I place myself at the disposal of the committee (is it a committee?) for whatever image they may choose.

Only, if I am to be bound to a certain size or a certain subject, I must know it as soon as possible, in order to think of my subject and enter into the spirit of it.

In short, I am sure you will arrange all this satisfactorily.

I send love and congratulations to the Princess.[1] Good-by. Your distinguished daughter,

ANDREY.[2]

[1] Her father's sister.

[2] Marie Bashkirtseff exhibited for the first time in the Salon of 1880, signing her picture Marie Courventin Reiss; in the Salon of the following year, 1881, she signed herself Andrey, a name which she often took in her correspondence. It was not until 1883, when she felt more confident of success, that she put her real name to her pictures.

To M. B——.

Dear B—— :

We spent the night at Bordeaux instead of at Bayonne and I write to tell you that we saw Sarah in *Camille*. Twenty-five francs for a seat in the balcony. She acted, it is needless to say, as only she can act, but I should criticise her support very sharply. Armand Duval was atrocious. And the costumes! At the risk of breaking your heart I will say that she was not well dressed; the gown in the first act was pretty enough; that in the second act (the blue), was pretty, also. The country costume was ugly and the ball dress uglier still. It had a horrible stiff garland which did not match the camellias at the bottom of the skirt at all. Of course for the provinces it was of no consequence; but all the same, if this dress cost what you say it did, Sarah was nicely cheated. And even if it had cost but a thousand francs it would still be ugly. I cannot understand how an artist like Sarah could wear such a thing. The last wrapper was charming, as was also the white pelisse.

As for her acting, it was divine. But there was something in her that did not go down with me; she looks too much like you. It is absurd to resemble another so strongly when one is not a relative.

Which of the two is the copy?

How are your two pensioners? Give them a great many messages from me. If you were amiable you would go again to 57*bis* Boulevard Rochechouart. You see I shall not rent a house till about the 15th of October, and I should be heartbroken if any one carried off this paradise, with its fine northern exposure, from me. Could you not, with the tact for which you are distinguished, arrange so that the *concierge* might let you know— I do not know just how, but in such a way as that I could breathe here freely without the fear of some painter (they are so base) hiring the studio I covet. If, in order to stimulate you to do this for me, it is necessary for me to say that the gown in the fourth act was pretty, I will willingly do so.

The weather is fine; it is warm. Biarritz is lovely, lovely.

To the Same.

BIARRITZ.

Dear B——:

The quatrain with which your letter begins would be worthy of you; it is charming. The gloves fit very well, and I thank you for them; that is three times two francs sixty-five centimes, that I owe you.

Yesterday Coquelin the younger played, and there was a great ball. There are only Spaniards and Russians here. The Spanish women are lovely, lovely, lovely; as for the Russian women there is only one and you know who she is.

It has rained for the last two days, and then it is the end of September; every one is taking flight, and we are going to make an art tour through Spain—a country for which I have an ardent admiration—without luggage, like the English; it is the most interesting country in Europe and one ought certainly to see it.

Do not regret not being at Biarritz, which is no livelier than Trouville or Aix; in your place I should take advantage of those charming Russians whom you know going to Spain, to make the journey under such delightful conditions. But I think truly, jesting apart, that you should make it; the season is altogether favorable, you have worked very hard, Paris is damp in October, you have a cough, you will be able to relate your Iberian, Castillian, and Andalusian adventures to Sarah—see how many considerations to induce your family to allow you to go, without counting that with a thousand times twenty sous the tour is performed as well as *Camille* is performed by Sarah. And then you will behave sensibly, being with a family party; and then, you will carry my painting utensils in the dangerous mountain passes where the squirrels or the hinds, it does not matter which, as they say at Victor Hugo's, scarcely dare venture. Think this dazzling project over, then, and good-by. Thanks from every one for the dogs and the studio; you are very sweet, as Madame Thiers used to say.

ANDREY,
Future grand medalist.

To the Same.

Dear and Illustrious B——:

Yes, I am in Spain and in a mantilla. I travel through the one wearing the other. I visit Toledo and the Escurial, making studies and conquests.

It is not impossible that I may paint some magnificent composition, but it is better not to expect too much. I think I can guess from Signor Juliano's hope of seeing me paint a great picture—I think I can guess, I say, that mamma has made a visit to the Signor Director and has instructed him to pretend he believes that I am painting here in order to make me remain in the South. If I am correct in attributing this Macchiavellian intention to your director, I shall withdraw my confidence from him and bestow it on Signor

Cot, who is not an accomplice of my family(!). You may tell him of this threat.

In any case, the time I remain in this ill-smelling country shall be employed in extracting their secrets from Velasquez, Rivera, and other the like scamps. And then, equipped with all this knowledge, I shall paint an immense picture from nature and annihilate Carolus, Tony and the other masters. Therefore, dear boy, I beg of you to make arrangements for removing the things from No. 37 (should the abominable proprietor put me out before January) by the 15th of October. I hope it will not be required. At all events it will be necessary to arrange things in Mlle. Oelnitz's old room. I expect to be back in three weeks, unless

—there are plenty of balconies, guitars, glances, and fan-flirtings; but work before everything.

I await your answer and sign myself humbly,

ANDREY,

Fabricator of masterpieces,
Successor to Velasquez,
Painter to several foreign courts,
And Professor of the Spanish language.

To M. *Julian.*

PICTURESQUE JOURNEY IN SPAIN.
By M. B. Andrey.

HOTEL DE PARIS, SEVILLE.

Dear Master:

O you, who perhaps intend one day to travel, follow my advice, the result of bitter experience.

In the matter of mothers, take the Mediterranean, and in the matter of aunts, her of the Travelers' Bazaar (Place de l'Opéra), for if you are in the least artistic, if you have the least tendency toward what the positivists call poetry, if you have some hidden corner in your soul which aspires toward something higher than a grocer's shop, were it even Gambetta's, if you set out with the idea of collecting sketches, studies, of seeing pictures—alas and alas! I am going to make you a participator, so to say, in my woful disappointments.

Burgos.—What is there here, then? Only a cathedral? One must be English to— Yes, I have heard it said that some English people went to Lausanne to see a cathedral. And how cold it is! Detestable country! And how pleasant it was at Biarritz, and why did we leave it? First douche.

Valladolid.—We did not stop here; they disgusted me with it by asking me twenty times before we reached it what was the name of the city at which I wished to stop next.

Madrid.—A capital, at least, and the air is pleasant, although the sun has set. But the museum is heated, I think. No matter, quick, quick! Let us go to Seville, where there are to be had good cow's milk and roast chicken, such as Marie loves, and then the climate there is very salubrious. Behold my dreams of Andalusia converted into a pectoral paste. Is it not allowable to hate people a little who disgust one in this way with what one was prepared to admire? But we shall soon go on to Seville, stopping to rest at Cordova, where the aloe and the cactus grow, and where the weather is warm. Delightful country! There were some complaints, however, at having no carriage, for this walk of ten yards and the visit to the mosque were going to exhaust me. Complaints in the third person. There was nothing to see. The guide had *invented* it all *on purpose* to make us lose the train.

Seville.—We went out to breathe the air and to take our bearings in the place, but we did not leave the principal streets, which are sheltered; the picturesque quarters, the streets broken up with squares and gardens, are frightful, on account of the wind.

The driver did it on *purpose.* Did

we by chance (a spiteful chance) come here to visit the suburbs of Seville?

I pray Heaven to render me indifferent to this pious trickery, but my patience is worn out. This constant practice of bringing everything down to a *bourgeois* level, from temperament; and of considering everything from a hygienic point of view, from principle, makes me wild; the more so as perhaps I am really ill. In any case, I have very unskillful physicians. In Madrid I was able to escape something of this, thanks to the museum and to our friends, among them a young artist who worked with us and with whose family we became acquainted here.

But traveling in a carriage people are obliged to remain together, and they are either continually interfering with one suggestion or another, for my benefit, or there is a dead silence. In default of community of thoughts and interests a little sprightliness at least would be necessary to make traveling in this manner tolerable, while I am like a person taking a walk who finds himself obliged to drag along cross and sleepy companions. Think which you would choose to accompany you to the Salon—one of your friends or the mother of any one of your pupils, I shall not specify which. Well, let your imagination complete the picture; for the short martyrdom of the *Salon* substitute an art journey (O mockery!) through romantic and picturesque Spain, and you will have a faint idea— I make the greatest efforts to preserve a certain amount of mental vigor, but even if I should force myself to bear it a little longer the spring is no longer there, the wings of the spirit droop and serve only to brush away my artistic projects and illusions, crumbled into dust under the hygienic pressure of those who love me. And as, contrariwise to our guide at Cordova and our driver at Seville, they do not do it *on purpose*, there is absolutely nothing to do but to fill a few sheets of paper with complaints and to send them to you, as if that could remedy anything.

But I cherish the secret hope* that you will send me here by the first courier some companion, like M. de Saint-Marceaux, sculptor, or M. Tony Robert-Fleury, painter. Was it not the intention of the latter to go this winter to Morocco? Tell him to hurry, since he must pass through Spain—the vessel sails from Cadiz.

> En partant du golfe d'Otrente,
>   Nous étions trente,
> Mais en arrivant à Cadiz,
>   Nous n'étions que dix.[1]

One would suffice for me. If Heaven does not send me some help you shall see me very soon.

End of a harrowing account of a journey through Spain by M. B. Andrey.

---

[1] When we left the Gulf of Otranto
   We were thirty,
But when we reached Cadiz
   We were only ten.

To her Mother.

34 Avenue Montaigne, Paris.
Dear Mamma:

I arrived here in very good condition.

Papa desires me to let you know that he has been quite well all this time. He will tell you about our adventures in Warsaw and Berlin.

The picture has been unpacked; they have made a hole in it which, fortunately, however, is scarcely noticeable. I have not yet had time to show it to any of the great artists.

Tony Robert-Fleury is well and is preparing to set out for Switzerland; up to the present I have seen only Julian, who is still stout, like C——, and who sends you a thousand remembrances. Mme. Gavini left Paris the day of my arrival, so that I have not seen her. Saint-Amand has gone to join his sister at Mont-Dore.

Paris is empty, but I have many things to occupy me, among others a picture for the *Salon*.

I send a number of things to Dina. Let her not complain of receiving so little. Papa cries like a cock on account of the custom-house, etc., etc. Papa cries like a peacock at the thought of being encumbered with so much luggage.

The commissions of the Princess have been executed.

With love; come soon to go to Biarritz.

To Mlle. Colignon.

My Dear Friend:

Here is my answer. It shall be a sort of disquisition on jealousy. Why on jealousy? I have not the slightest idea. Jealousy and monarchy are my favorite subjects. Can there be anything in the world more absurd than jealousy! One makes one's self ridiculous by being jealous. You love a woman, she loves you; one fine day she ceases to love you, but is that her fault? Does she love you no longer because she wishes to love you no longer? Did she love you because she wished to love you? No. Well, then, why torture her? Why this stupid, useless rage? For a woman or a man cast aside and replaced by another woman or man, say what you will, is always pitiable. And the ridiculous part one plays is badly disguised by the grand tragic robe. One's love changes or one loves another, but this is not because one wishes it to be so. It is an incomprehensible, involuntary change, produced, doubtless, by the changes in the molecules of the imagination. If one is so jealous as to be unable to bear his jealousy any longer, why, let him kill them both, and himself afterward.

I often ask myself if there can be anything in the world more disgusting or more ridiculous than jealousy. When one is jealous without cause, in spite of everything there remains a doubt in the mind; one should then go to the woman and entreat her in the name of all she holds dear and sacred to set this doubt at rest ; it is true that one is made very miserable by doing so, for women are great wretches and are always ready to torture those who throw themselves frankly on their mercy.

My disquisition being ended—a disquisition which for the first time in my life faithfully expresses my thoughts— I embrace you, and await your reply.

1882.

To her Mother.

Villa Misé Brun, Nice.

Dear Mamma:

We arrived safely, everything is charming, and I am delighted to be here. We are in very good spirits, the weather is very fine, and all I fear is that my dear family will come with their habitual bickerings. We are so tranquil, so sensible! Paul, Sacha, and Dina overwhelm me with attentions. Vassili cooks very well. Rosalie waits on us with zeal; the sun warms. In short, everything goes on satisfactorily in this best of worlds. Seize the occasion, quickly, then, and come before the carnival ; everything is ready for your reception.

Send me immediately the white Algerian burnouse, which is on the top of the wardrobe in my bedroom, the parasol lined with pink, and the black gown trimmed with black feathers, which are in the press in the dressing-room.

A thousand kind remembrances to everybody.

And, above all, touch none of my books or the pictures which are on top of the books. Let the dust lie. Do not disturb the least scrap of paper, I beg of you.

To the Same.

JOUY-EN-JOSAS.

Dear Mother:

I have been for the last three days with the Canroberts; I can give you

There will neither be amusements, nor an opportunity to do anything, if he is ill and low-spirited.

I should like to go to Algeria. That would be advisable for many reasons; I should have the author of my being to nurse, and my picture to paint. You see that would suit me admirably.

But if, as is more likely, I do not make the journey,—and I should not regret not doing so,—return as soon as possible, and bring with you the money to pay for my portrait. You must act in accordance with the tenor of my first letter, the one which contains my recommendations, and in which I ask you to return quickly.

Answer by telegraph. Bring my father back with you, since he requires nursing; tell the Princess that if he reno idea of their kindness; the Maréchale herself arranged the covers of my bed; they are adorable people. And the place is very pretty and quite near Versailles. Settle matters soon. I send you a kiss.

To the Same.

Mamma:

As you have had that fire, and as papa is ill, I see plainly that my projects are no longer feasible. Examine the question and tell me frankly what you think. Consider the folly, the enormity of taking such a journey at this season. And, above all, if papa is ill, and the physicians recommend a milder climate for him, it would be madness on his part to remain there.

mains in the country, ill as he is, he will die.

I await your answer to my last letter and the present one, but I am convinced that you will come, for, under present circumstances, for me to undertake the journey would be the act of a mad woman.

Love to every one.

To M. Julian.

Dear Master :

So much has been said about the rights of women and so many intelligent and learned people have treated the subject with ridicule that one is almost ashamed even to mention the subject ; and yet the rights and the equality we claim have nothing to do with politics, and have no connection whatever either with nihilism, or socialism, or Bonapartism, or the right to vote, or the eligibility of women to public office.

All these questions have been everywhere agitated; many instances of the injustice with which the weaker sex is treated have been brought forward; there is one, however, that has been mentioned by no one, perhaps because it is the most real, the most striking, and the most cruel of all—the absence of a School of Fine Arts for women.

How comes it, foreigners ask in wonder, that women are admitted to the School of Medicine, and that the School of Fine Arts is closed against them? At St. Petersburg, at Stockholm women are received at the Academy, and neither city pretends to be the equal of Paris!

Exactly, many say to us; and this is the best argument that can be used against you; in France, in Paris, such a thing would not be possible.

And why not, we ask?

To this they respond by a long discourse, under three heads, bristling with conclusions, all going to prove that our society is rotten and that the immorality of the French nation is such that what would be practicable elsewhere would not be at all practicable in France. And we retort by repeating, in the first place, that women are admitted to the School of Medicine—we will afterward specify the branches they are allowed to study—and that in the School of Fine Arts (as in the countries we have mentioned) they come in contact with the men pupils. The æsthetic course is pursued by both sexes together only in Sweden. And since in France women and men attend the various courses together, in what respect would these courses be more dangerous or more objectionable if pursued at the school? The studios in which they work with the model are separate.

So that they are separated in the only study in which it might be objectionable to have them together.

The model in the men's class is nude; in that of the women he wears drawers like those worn by the bathers at Trouville and Dieppe, whom the most modest of ladies do not scruple to look at. So that, while the pupils are separated where it would be objectionable for them to study together, they are together where it would be to their advantage to be so.

Great publicity is given to the competition for admission and to the expulsions, which contributes not a little to the maintenance of order at the school.

The legend of the woman artist, of that vagabond and perverted being without industry or talent,—repulsive, hungry, beautiful,—who always comes to a bad end, is a story in which little faith is placed now, although it has been the custom to cloak under the noble and honored name of *artist* a multitude of things which for the most part bear no relation to art. The old prejudice, however, has only been replaced by an excessively vague idea of what would be possible. The type is no longer grotesque, it no longer possesses any interest. It is not the few individuals who come under our notice, the charlatans, the young ladies who make copies at the Louvre or who have learned to paint pretty pictures in fashionable studios, who can enlighten us on this point. It is at the multitude, embracing a not inconsiderable number of talented pupils, who study art seriously in private studios— it is at this large number, who have really an amount of talent which would astonish those who ridicule the work of women, that we must look if we would know how interesting these workers are and by means of what incredible labors they succeed in acquiring a tolerably good education, faulty though it may be in many respects.

The studio of M. X——, which is the studio most numerously attended, contains more than fifty pupils.

Those who scoff at feminine talent can never know how many women who have taken up art seriously, women of genuine and remarkable talent, have been discouraged and their talents wasted through a vicious or incomplete education. The woman artist is quite as interesting as the man artist. It may be said that with two or three exceptions there has been no example of a woman having produced any work of art comparable to the best work of men artists. Yes, but the men receive, in one of the best schools in the world, an intelligent and comprehensive education; during the whole day they are surrounded by works of art, their eyes rest only on pure lines and brilliant colors, they breathe an atmosphere that opens their souls to inspiration and develops the wings of their imagination, on which they may soar to the heights of genius. And for women, nothing; or the chance of private studios.

What is there surprising, then, in the fact that with two or three exceptions there have never been women artists of real importance. And why this injustice toward woman, who has proved herself a thousand times more courageous, more persevering, obliged as she is to struggle not only against the poverty—unhappily common to both male and female artists—but also against terrible prejudices and difficulties without number, lacking even the freedom of movement which men have?

It is to man, who by his very nature has all the facilities for study, that all the means are given; and to woman, whom nature has deprived of freedom of movement and who has to struggle against everything, that this instruction is denied. There are too many women artists already, it may be said; woman was made for home. Alas, it is not by depriving them of the means of satisfying a noble passion that they will be inspired with a desire to spin wool. Why not afford women of ambition this glorious outlet? Why not encourage these aspirations toward the great, the beautiful, the useful, by making Paris the capital of the world, which like ancient Rome claims to be the *curia dignitatis gymnasium litterarum, domicilium verborum mundi, patriam libertatis?*

To accomplish this an appeal should be made to all artists.

But these are not serious objections; and if they were the only ones nothing would be easier than to establish two studios of thirty or forty pupils each; there are facilities in plenty. But that would displease Messieurs the professors, in the first place, because it would be an innovation, a change, and routine is one of the flowers which thrives best in our institutes—and then, women! It is not worth thinking seriously about. Would it be possible for a woman to work seriously? Yes, she can work seriously, and there are even many who think she can, while saying to the contrary. But what would you have? It is so common to look down upon women. It is so common that it should cease to be practiced, and that it should be considered better taste not to do so.

It is to persons of enlightenment, to artists, to the disciples of art, who see only pure lines and brilliant colors, who breathe an atmosphere that opens the soul to the inspiration of what is puissant and beautiful, and develops the wings of the imagination on which they may soar to the heights of genius—it is to the friends of progress and of justice, that an appeal should be made.

France has a genius for painting.

To M. B——.

Dear B—— :

My answer goes to you from the heart of Poltava, where we are performing deeds of prowess in the chase, in comparison with which the exploits of the renowned Nimrod sink into insignificance. The weather is still fine, and a lunch in the woods, at a distance of two hours' journey from any dwelling, is something very *chic*.

The day before yesterday, Sunday, we killed twenty-seven wolves, seventeen foxes, and two hundred and sixty-three hares. I have on my conscience only four wolves and a fox; you will see them at the Rue Ampère, where we shall be about the 3d of September. I hope that you have returned to Babylon, and that Brittany mourns your absence. Papa wrote to Alexis to invite him to the hunt, but has received no answer from him.

What have you done with your family, Bojidar—cheologus? What a pity it is that we are so far away! With some friends from Lutetia one could enjoy one's self so well. Tell Alexis that his *fiancée*, Julie, is charming; she will be fourteen in a month.

The future parents-in-law of Alexis-miletis entertained us for three days with a magnificence which plainly indicates that, so far as the dowry is concerned, Balthazar, Sardanapalus, and M. Grévy are as nothing compared to Alexandre; and this, joking apart. But notwithstanding everything I feel the need of saturating myself with civilization and with painting.

Every one sends love.

Good-by for a while.

How is Sergeant Hoff?

God keep you. Regards to——.

To M. Julian.

In order not to dispute with you *viva voce*, dear director, I write to you; otherwise it would be impossible for me to preserve the necessary calmness.

In my desire to find an explanation of the persistent discouragement you heap upon me with such delightful calmness, I form many conjectures. Perhaps I have lost my mind, like the *Greco* or like Madame O'Connell, and am painting locomotives and cathedrals for human faces; in that case it would be necessary to take serious steps to prevent me from running about loose. Or perhaps you think that all the flatteries I receive have made me inordinately conceited, and that at all costs it is necessary to take down my pride.

Or perhaps——

But you know well that I do not believe at all, at all, in your candor; *you know* that I judge myself impartially, and that I am much more than discouraged; a discouragement to which you have contributed with a thirty-six horse power, but for which I bear you no ill will. Why do you keep up the farce of pretending to believe me blinded and crazed by vanity? Why do you torture me by maddening warnings? If it is to put me beside myself, you have succeeded; in future I shall try not to listen to your perfidious advice; that is all.

But if it is for my good, know that you deceive yourself, and most disastrously so for me. When one desires to help people, when one really thinks they are in danger of drowning, one does not amuse one's self by filling their pockets with lead.

Besides, you do not believe a word of what you say when you talk about studies made at home or out of doors, which you make up into a bundle, perfidiously call pictures, and then use to crush me.

Have you, then, ever thrown in the faces of your X———'s, and other shining lights, their academic figures and their casts? My *pictures* are no worse than those, only that I would at any time rather *fail* in a sincere and interesting study than succeed in a model, the more so as the knowledge acquired is the same in both; the process only is different.

That I have not reached my aim, that I am not a master, that I have still a great deal to learn, is evident; but between that and coming to tell me that I know not what terrible catastrophe has happened, that I can no longer do anything—that all is over—there is a great difference.

What I have produced is not much; but, after all, the pictures are there and they were not painted by the cook of the *Café Anglais* to amuse himself. As a *result* they count for nothing; but they are studies as good as any other studies; and then, since you keep such exact records, consult those records, and you will see that I have not even had the necessary time to pass through all the phases of decadence, through which the individuals whom you so often cite have passed.

Deducting the time lost by illness, I have spent three years painting. This is an age for my impatience, but judging dispassionately, it is not long. So you see everything is opposed—the time I have spent in painting and my own inclination—to my accepting the rôle of retired pupil, which you wish to confer upon me.

The first of what you treacherously call my paintings was done in 1880, after eighteen months' study, during

twelve months only of which I worked all day. The last was done in the spring of 1882, during convalescence after an illness, when I had fever at least once a week. In the interval I exhibited the very mediocre "Atelier"[1] (without mention); and according to what even your most hostile young ladies say, I have rather improved than gone back since then. This brings me to that silly nonsense about exhibiting which you seem to regard as an impossibility. I should perhaps make as honorable an appearance at the Salon as Miss K——, otherwise it would be necessary to return to the supposition that I am mad, *à la Greco.*

[1] "Un Atelier," signed Andrey, a picture exhibited at the Salon, representing the Studio Julian.

The more I think about it, the more I am convinced that you must have some inexplicable motive in seeking to crush me. You seem positively to delight in heaping discouragements of the most torturing kind upon me. It is plain that you do not consider what a terrible, I might almost say what a criminal thing it is to say to one who passionately longs to learn and study, "You! You can do nothing more!" It is a moral assassination, more cruel than the assassination of the body, for you repeat it daily.

If you have any object in this, I cannot discover what it is. To affirm brutally that I can do nothing more is a very serious matter, and, in short—you know nothing about it. It will only result in a paralysis of the faculties and eight pages of literature. How will that profit you?

Now, outside the art question, for which I hate you, for you have here done me the greatest possible injury, we are good friends, and the proof of it is that on Saturday you dine at the Rue Ampère.

1883.

To Mlle. ——.[1]

My Dear Little Alice:

I was very glad receiving your nice letter. I am coming back very soon; you may expect to see me at eight o'clock Monday, the 10th of April, at the blessed atelier Julian.

The picture I was doing for the Salon is not yet finished. You may well understand that I can have no pleasure in sending something that is not entirely good, at least that is not as good as I may do.

I am flattered by the admiration of B——; you find her intelligent; she is

---

[1] This letter is a transcript of the original, which is in English.

so, but when you know her better you will see that the first days she looks more than she is in reality.

Besides she is not good, and with all the appearances of brutal frankness she knows what it is to be false when she needs it.

As to her talent she has it, but not so much as she imagines herself; besides she is full of German vanity. Now *l'éreintement* est aussi complet que possible. Do not think I think bad of her; it is merely the love of *analysis* that makes me look into people's nature more than it would perhaps be suitable. B—— has des défauts mais elle a aussi des qualités, unfortunately one cannot say so of many.

As to the picture, *canaille*, it would

not be yet bad to do it, if there were talent.

Good-by; if you will see some one's pictures before the Salon, tell me what is it. I stay here eight days more.

Sincerely yours,
ANDREY.

Is not my letter very wicked? The truth is seldom agreeable and nearly always we dare not tell it not to be accused of jealousy.

To Mlle. ——.

RUE AMPÈRE.

Dear Friend:

There was once a studio filled with young ladies and married ladies, among whom were a Russian and an

American. The Russian conceived a friendship for the American and was exceedingly kind to her, trying to make herself agreeable to her on every occasion, without considering that there are many people who think one can never do a kindness to any one without having some selfish motive. That this reflection, not very flattering to the person concerning whom it is made, is made very often, the greatest moralists affirm.

Be this as it may, the Russian treated the American like a little sister, saying before her all the childish nonsense that came into her head. An aristocrat by nature, she committed the mistake perhaps of supposing that it would be taken for granted that an artist was not for her a man; and she spoke of artists as one speaks of a favorite race horse or of a singer, concerning whom the most insignificant details are interesting.

And as she admitted her friend to a share in these pleasantries, a thought occurred to the American, of which, were I in her place, I should be eternally ashamed. It was that the Russian made use of her to avoid compromising herself, and one fine day she made a remark to the Russian which absolutely astounded the latter, so that she did not know what to answer. The answer she should have given was to turn her back on the little American, but not having the presence of mind to do this instantly, she reflected afterward that it would be unworthy of her to attach any importance to a silly impertinence, and she resolved to treat the whole matter with good-humored contempt. My opinion is that she was wrong; and then this course of conduct was not understood by the American, who assumed ridiculous airs of importance, owing to the fact that a great lady and her daughter had manifested an interest in her, by which her head was a little turned, so that it never occurred to her that her conduct, after the manner in which she had been treated by the family of the Russian, might, perhaps, in the eyes of many persons, redound to her discredit.

But to conclude. As the Russian is exceedingly tolerant in her disposition, and as her thoughts are occupied with serious matters rather than with nonsense of this kind, she took the affair philosophically, thinking it all very natural, and contenting herself with laughing a little at it satirically, like the "Harlequin" of Saint Marceaux, an artist whom she esteems and whose genius she admires.

I hope, my dear Alice, that you, too, will laugh a little at this history, which is as instructive as it is amusing, and which I relate to you because I do not think it well that I should be always taken for a fool.

Mlle. Canrobert has given me your address, which gives me an opportunity of wishing you every sort of happiness in America. You already know, doubtless, that I have obtained a mention.

Do not forget, above all, to give me

news of the picture of M. Bastien-Lepage, an artist whom I esteem and whose genius I admire.

A thousand regards.

MARIE.

P. S.—If you should chance to meet the little American of my story, tell her not to trouble herself to slander the Russian in order to excuse her stupidity; the Russian will not take the trouble to turn her into ridicule.

To Mlle. ——.

30 RUE AMPÈRE,
(BOULEVARD MALESHERBES.)

My Dear Alice:

I am glad for you if you like Pont-Aven, only you know I am not an admirer of the celebrated Britain, because all the artists that go there bring back studies which all seem to come from the same shop, with the difference of qualities—first, second, third, and eleventh. It is love. If one or two can do something of a fisherwoman, six hundred and seventy-three produce——

Art is something more than the fashion to paint anything *en plein air*. Bastien himself thinks so.

As to the brother's portrait, it is not finished; we wait the return from the country of Miss F——.

Now, my *grand tableau* is a secret, of course. I am working at its preparation and write while the model reposes. It is not the preparation, as we say at Julian's. I am only doing studies, for it must not be done in an atelier. Well, I was going to tell the great secret.

I am glad to hear Miss Webb does good things. She is nice; *mes très sincères amitiés* to her and Miss B——.

You cannot imagine the *scie* that became my pastel; it is so very good, every one speaks of it to my friends who come to me and say what they have heard. I am quite sorry it is not a picture. Bastien says that it is art even if it were a mere *fusain*. M. Lefevre saw it, and M. Tony asked me to give it for his atelier; but it is a portrait and cannot be given like that; then he said he would pose himself.

Les orgues et les voix de femmes! Remember Carolus painted by Sargent. Goodness, *non sum dignus!*

Well, now, *plaisanterie à part*, I am happy to be of the illustrious *atelier des dames*. Some—suppose few—were so wicked, and I feel unfortunately so deeply the antipathy! One is enough to vitiate the air of a whole room. I am sure now that I made few progress, partly because I paid too much attention to those delightful *voix de femmes*, whose judgments paralyzed what I was to do; indeed, when I was painting there was always the thought that they disprized my work. It is very stupid, I know — especially because they said of me what they said of artists whose shoes are too high-born to be blacked by them. Some sweet women's voices say Bastien is not an artist, but only *un exécutant!*

Perhaps we shall go to Dieppe; if

you are still there I will come and see you; only I am afraid[1] to be captivated by that Brittany that I despised, and regret too much not having gone there to work.

I must stop now, or I shall enter on a series of considerations as to what is to be preferred—what I prefer, what we must strive after—

The composition, the idea, the sentiment, or—

Do we know?

Happy they who are not artists. One must be mad to enlist in this army of tortured spirits. But once one has entered it, one never deserts it.

I remember the picture of M. Sim-

---

[1] Thus far in English, in the original; the rest of the letter is in French.

mons. He is a man of taste *in every sense.*

Good-by. I see I am writing in French now, and I must stop or I shall go on in Italian.

I am, my sweet friend, with love, sincerely and cordially yours.

When I had closed this letter and was writing the address, I was seized with a wild desire to go and work on the seashore. There is no use in being shut up in a studio of any kind. I should like to follow my letter. I fancy I feel the sea breezes blowing through my hair—voices of women, organ-tones. If it were not for this frightful picture! But in any case I shall go. I shall arrive—at least, unless I change my mind.

To M. B——.

B——! How absurd you are to be so greatly disturbed about nothing.

As a thousand artistic complications prevent my leaving the house I write to you instead of going to soothe your woes by my presence. To say I have no heart! You know that mamma is gone away and that consequently you are not the only obstacle to the representation. But at the same time that this has disarranged everything it arranges many things in regard to painting. When you are able to come here you shall see some fine pictures.

I advise you to work in plaster as an amusement while you are in bed. At least the loss of time would not be very great.

Four days ago we received a visit from some great artists who think well of you and who exclaimed, when they saw your portrait, "Why, look, B——!"

I am waiting for Mlle. de V——; my *gamins* have not come; it is a superb rainy day, notwithstanding the sun, and, as a return to former times, I have taken up an old habit. You like to quarrel; I am too busy with my large picture for such nonsense. But you love the fine arts too well to reproach me greatly for this.

Good-by. I must stop, for Coco and Prater are beginning their racket again.

Marie-Chesse.

To M. Alexander D——.

Monsieur:

I am told that, like every self-respecting divinity, you are enveloped in a cloud which makes you regard the inhabitants of the earth with indifference.

I do not believe this, for the cloud in question is generally only a fog which gathers around the minds of those who are growing old; and you, Monsieur, can never grow old.

But, philosopher or demi-god though you be, it is impossible that you should refuse me what I am going to ask of you; impossible, because in the first place I desire it with all my heart, and in the next place it will cost you nothing.

What I ask is that you should be for once the spiritual director of a woman who desires to consult you, as she would a priest, regarding a very serious matter. But reassure yourself, Monsieur and illustrious man; I have not the slightest intention of recounting to you "the romance of my life," or anything else that would affect your nerves.

I come somewhat late, I know, and I tremble to think of the numbers of those who must have written to you about similar things; but that is not my fault.

In your books you seem to be as great and as good as it is possible to be, and if you show yourself scornful now you will destroy one of my most cherished illusions; and when there is no need of committing an action like this it is better to avoid doing so. If, then, you show yourself kind and sympathetic, and possessed of that goodness of heart characteristic of men of genius (I do not wish to flatter you, but it is necessary that you should know why I bend the knee before you and write to you in this humble style), if, then, you are as good as I imagine you to be, come on Thursday, March 20, to the ball at the Opera House, the only place where I can see you. Write me a line in answer, to the post-office of the Madeleine, for you can understand that if you are not to be there I will not go.

If you are Olympic, however, if you have grown *bourgeois*, stay at home, for in truth you inspire me with a sacred awe, and I should be unable to utter a word in your presence.

I should like to say to you that I am a woman *comme il faut*, but that would make you think the contrary.

As this document is in my handwriting it would be very amiable of you to return it to me.

To the Same.

You are right; novel reading has turned my head. Such things should not be done.

I cried with anger at your thinking what you did, but I was in truth too silly. You are not the man to whom to send foolish epistles, copied by a public scribe.

It is an escapade, however, which

has caused me not a little unhappiness!

At all events, I assure you that I was not deceiving you; that, finding myself face to face with a situation from which I saw no way of extricating myself, forced to take a desperate resolution, I prayed to God, and I then thought of you, fancying you might be the rare being who, instead of taking me for one of " those women of the world who, etc.," would understand that a soul in torment had come to you for light.

You make me feel forcibly the difference that exists between what we imagine and what really is. I will keep early hours, I promise you; thus, thanks to you, I shall always remain young.

As to the guidance of which I stand in need I shall ask it from Him who suggested to me the thought of asking it from you.

Sleep well, Monsieur, and continue to be as much a *bourgeois* in private as you are an artist for the public; that too is an excellent method of keeping from growing old.

I shall see you doubtless on Saturday at the Chamber. The divorce law will be proposed.

Apropos of divorces, I announce to you now that of my admiration from your person.

To M——.

30 RUE AMPÈRE, PARIS.

Dear Master:

What is painting, however beautiful, however grand, after seeing the "Harlequin[1] of Saint Marceaux"? Mean, artificial, false, the decadence of art! Who is the critic who has justly described this statue? Who is the writer of genius who has called the attention of the public to this astonishing work? Who is the Théophile Gautier who is to explain its beauties to the people, placing this extraordinary work in its true light? It is very difficult, in our times, to speak with justice of an artist who is living and who is still young. And I do not think that the critics will

---

[1] A statue by Saint Marceaux.

dare to place any one, whoever he may be, above—every one else.

And then the public has learned to regard certain names as representing the whole sum of human genius,— Phidias, Michael Angelo, and Raphael, and a few others of later date,—so that an authority and, above all, an independence of mind, which are not to be found, would be needed thus to proclaim the supremacy of a contemporary work.

The "Harlequin" is not only unrivaled in execution but it is also, and above all, a highly philosophical work. Can it be possible that the public will perceive only the freedom, the skill, the talent it reveals? It is true that its execution alone would make it a master-piece, but the idea it embodies, and its breadth of treatment render it a conception of the highest order. It is the highest expression of genius, of the comic and satirical order. It is the most delicate, the most complete, and the grandest representation of the superior mind passing in review the vices, the follies, and the basenesses of humanity. There is an excess of vigor in it, which is characteristic of our epoch. It is delicate, it is profound, it is awful, it is sublime.

The sublime allegory trembles, vibrates; the muscles quiver under the close-fitting garments. Standing firmly on his feet, the head thrown boldly back, the arms folded, his wand in his hand, the mouth laughing scornfully, the clown satirizes humanity.

Go look at M. X. Y. Z.'s work; it is

very fine; it has beautiful lines, living flesh; it shows great ability. Then look at the work of Saint Marceaux; go back again to the other and you will receive an impression of hollowness, weakness, as when one looks at a decorative panel after seeing a fine painting.

To her Brother.

30 RUE AMPÈRE, PARIS, May.
Dear Paul:

What has happened to you that you do not write to me? I think you might at least send me a few words on the occasion of my honorable mention. Write to me about everything and especially about the health of papa. What do the doctors say, *seriously speaking?*

We go out very little; I am painting a new picture in our garden, and that takes up all my time; last Sunday we went to see the people returning from the Grand Prix; it was a fine sight and the weather was superb.

For some days past I have been in a very bad humor, and we have received no one; besides, the weather is very warm and some people have gone to the country, not many, for the greater number remain here until it is time to go to the seashore. I shall wait until mamma returns and does what I have asked her. Coco and Prater have been fighting with each other all day; that is all the news there is to tell you.

Give my love to your wife and the children. But you do not know what has happened to us! Louis, the negro boy is to make his first communion to-morrow, and lo! the priest has just discovered that he has never been baptized. So I sent everywhere in haste to look for a godfather, and as the matter was very urgent and no one was at home, we had to get the sacristan to take the place of papa, whose name I had registered as godfather. I named him Louis-Jules-René-Marie, and the priest pronounced a discourse, saying that this baby of fourteen was now under my protection and that I was his spiritual mother. The boy spent the whole evening in retreat, and to-morrow B—— will take him to the church to make his first communion. Can you not fancy you see B—— in this rôle? They did not remove any of his clothing for the baptism, but simply poured a little water on his head, put some salt on his tongue, and anointed his forehead, his neck, etc., with oil, as we do.

Behold, then, Louis-Jules-René-Marie a Christian, and to-morrow he will take communion.

This is the great event. Good-by.

Regards and love to yourself. Remembrances to everybody.

To Mlle. Canrobert.

SATURDAY, June 21.

Dear Claire:

We have had a storm accompanied by rain.

The painting was injured but not irreparably. At heart I am delighted.

It happened about four o'clock, at the very instant when I was *seized* with the idea of making a composition in clay. It was an inspiration from Heaven and it has plunged me into a state of ineffable joy. I was perfectly happy for two hours. Love, when it is reciprocated, must produce a somewhat similar feeling. I scarcely took the time to make a sketch before attacking the clay. One must neither think nor experiment—the fingers execute a *prescribed* work with mechanical precision. I *saw* and I executed.

As it is possible that the occasion I speak of may have an influence on my whole life, I will describe it to you in detail. I first made a hasty sketch, which did not interpret my thought. Instead of making a fresh attempt, which is always a loss of time, I began to read Jeanne d'Arc, and it was on the cover of this book that I sketched in an instant the composition, of which no important detail is to be changed. It descends like a hurricane. (It is a bas-relief.) The figures in the foreground are in high relief. The background is barely sketched in. It is to be very large—life-size—with 17 or 18 figures. It is a furious descent, an invasion, a storm of youth. It comes on you like a whirlwind. Spring is represented as a youthful god rushing forward, followed by a crowd of young girls and youths; they almost fly. It begins in the background to the left and comes forward and down toward the right where Spring stands; at his feet are children, eagerly gathering flowers; to his left a young girl is running and trying to look in his face; behind him a young man and a young woman are standing close together, gazing at each other; slightly bent down, the face of the young woman is almost concealed. Behind her a young girl is stooping down to rouse from sleep a younger girl, who is rubbing her eyes; boys with their arms raised in air sing and laugh, and in the background some women are laughing at an old man sitting crouched at the foot of a tree; a Cupid resting on this tree is tickling the old man's shoulder with a branch.

To her Mother.

30 RUE AMPÈRE, PARIS.

Dear Mamma:

Buy me a complete history of Russia, from the remotest times; and, in addition, a work on the costumes, architecture, and furniture of the ancient Russians, their customs, etc.—one in which I shall be able to find everything bearing on the subject, and if you are to remain long in Russia, send them to me. And do not forget, dear mamma, what I have written in my preceding letters.

P. S.—I want a history of Russia which contains all the legends of antiquity. Do not buy Solovieff's history, in one volume, for I have it already.

I send you my love,

Write to the Maréchale.

1884.

To M. B——.

My Dear B——:

Since custom requires that I should address a few words to you which will only bore you—here they are. But even without my writing you must still have been convinced that you would always meet with profound sympathy from me and from my family on the occasion of any happy or unhappy event in your family.

Your poor father suffered greatly and his malady was an incurable one; this should be a consolation to you, if there can be consolation for such a loss. We must only be brave; life is a tissue of miseries. I say this now as I have said it in my gayest moments. Embrace your dear mother for us all. Give a clasp of the hand to Alexis, and believe me sincerely your friend.

P. S.—Give us news of everything.

To Mlle. ——.

Dear Claire:

I have found my picture, but—— that is to say, it is entirely *suitable*, and I think it is interesting, but do not speak of it to any one, and *do not ask me what it is.* I am working in a retired corner at Saint Cloud and no one is to know anything about it. This is because, in the first place—of the evil eye.

And in the next, because the great Bastien-Lepage has said to me that if

I do not isolate myself like a cholera patient, I shall never accomplish my *best*.

You know that I have an unbounded admiration for this great man.

I have therefore secluded myself even from my family. But as I have some friends living near Versailles whom I have set my mind on seeing, I am going to do something unheard-of, wonderful! Yes! I am going to take an entire week from my picture and we shall make copies of Cazin together. If you knew how complicated a work my picture is you would thank me for this—I will not say sacrifice, since it is a pleasure for me; supply the word yourself.

Do not expire with joy then when I tell you that you will have me with you for seven entire days, for it is probable that I will give you seven more days later on, if I should become so disgusted with my picture as to be forced to remain for a while without looking at it. Next Monday, then, I shall take the 10.25 train at the little station at Jouy, *without fail.* But be an angel, and if the barometer should fall let me know of it beforehand, so that I may defer my visit—on account of the Cazins. I am coming to make you work, and work hard.

What do you say to the handwriting and the style of this letter? The truth is that the work which is in preparation demands all my energy. I must not waste any of it.

Ah, painting!

To the Same.

You must tell me, my dear Claire, the exact source of *Jonas*.[1] Those two verses tormented me so greatly that I thought of composing a continuation, as Michael Angelo thought of putting legs to the famous antique torso. I must learn then, precisely where you found " Jonas seated in his whale." If the verses are your own,

---

[1] The two first lines are by Mlle. C.——, the others by Marie Bashkirtseff.

> Jonas assis dans sa baleine
> Disait : Ah, que je voudrais sortir
> On a beau avoir des loisirs,
> Rester ici me fait de la peine.
> M'y v'la depuis tantôt trois jours
> Je commence à la trouver sévère
> J'suis séparé de mes amours,
> Je veux m'en aller de ma mère,
> D'attant plus qu'mon angoisse est énorme,
> Car enfin si jamais je suis dehors,

say so frankly, for they are very fine, and at our next interview I will recite for you my continuation, for that too is very fine. I have found my model again, but I have—— Secrecy and discretion.

"Work, take pains——"

I should like to see this picture already painted.

A thousand regards.

> C'est que cette carcasse difforme
> M'aura rendu au pis encore.
> Il en était là d'son monologue
> Quand un grand bruit se fit soudain,
> C'étaient de très habiles marins,
> Qui s'amenaient sur une pirogue,
> La baleine saisie d'effroi
> Jeta l'prophète à la dérive,
> Et obligée, mais pleine d'émoi
> Nagea vite vers une autre rive.
> C'est ainsi que finit l'aventure,
> Jonas qui était très fort
> Se fit mettre dans les Écritures
> Et envoya une note au Sport.

To her Brother.

30 Rue Ampère, Paris.
Sunday, February 30.

Dear Paul:

It is almost two o'clock, and I write to you in bed, after returning from the *Italians,* where I heard Massenet's "Hérodiade." I went with the maréchale and Claire.

Ah! what divine art! what genius! What sublimity, what beauty! The first act surprises by the novelty and the grandeur of its harmonies. It resembles nothing I have ever heard. It is truly original—full, sonorous, and harmonious. One can listen to the opera from beginning to end with undiminished delight. The music and the words blend together; there is an absence of *arias,* of middle harmonies.

There is sweep, breadth, magnificence, grandeur in it. Massenet is undoubtedly a great artist, and henceforth to be counted among the glories of France. It is said that the beauties of a fine musical composition cannot be understood at once. Well, one can understand at once that this work is admirable and melodious, notwithstanding an extremely scientific orchestration.

There is an accompaniment at the end of the first act so beautiful that I was transported by it. And several times we looked at one another with eyes filled with tears of enthusiasm. If the audience had followed their impulses they would have wept, so powerful, so affecting, so grand are some of its passages.

The enthusiasm was universal. It was a triumph, and Jules Massenet must be a happy man. Doubtless, if I were to hear it a second time I should find it still more beautiful; but I will not admit that one cannot understand truly fine music, hearing it for the first time.

The appearance of *John the Baptist* in the first act was thrilling. In the *aria* of *Herod* and the *duo* of *John* and *Salome* there were bursts of melody which made the enthusiasm of the audience rise to its highest pitch.

The maréchale wore a diamond ornament—an eagle holding an olive branch in its beak. The Empire is peace. But she thought the opera admirable. It was so.

Doubtless *my* Italian music will not bear comparison with this dazzling work, for this is so admirable as to be almost overpowering—no, not that. And it is with an orchestration in two tones that Italian romances move one most profoundly. The old airs of the old operas. And "Aïda"—well, it is a little like "Hérodiade"; but Massenet is a melodious French Wagner. No, Manet is Wagner rather. He is the father, to some extent, of the *new school*, of those for whom science takes the place of truth and feeling. There have always been new schools.

I ask your pardon for having overpraised "Hérodiade." The poem, in the first place, is not good ; and then, and then——

To M——.

I might answer you in your own words—" They are all asses."

What is certain is that the plans which have been accepted are all inferior to yours, which is in a pure and elevated style of art. Those imbeciles have selected figures suitable for statuary.

I know that any words I could say would be powerless to console you, and that you must be almost on the brink of despair.

When one misses an opportunity one is apt to fancy that another will never present itself. And the more one thinks about the disappointment the more enraged one becomes. Afterward one recovers one's serenity and makes up for what one has missed, for one can do this with a determined will. This is what one must be well persuaded of. Weak natures bewail the past; those who have energy and intelligence make the future a past. These are not idle w are the truth.

Throw your chagrin out of the railway carriage and back. And then they will gin over again. They ca Paris with the D—— col F—— cubes. It will be get the work and in retu make a monument for me dead.

Meantime, amuse you back your painter restore and all will go well. Pa at the coming Salon, we triumph.

I can no longer make

[1] See the letter reproduced

be almost overpowering—no, not that. And it is with an orchestration in two tones that Italian romances move one most profoundly. The old airs of the old operas. And "Aïda"—well, it is a little like "Hérodiade"; but Massenet is a melodious French Wagner. No, Manet is Wagner rather. He is the father, to some extent, of the *new school*, of those for whom science takes the place of truth and feeling. There have always been new schools.

I ask your pardon for having overpraised "Hérodiade." The poem, in the first place, is not good; and then, and then——

To M——.

I might answer you in your own words—"They are all asses."

What is certain is that the plans which have been accepted are all inferior to yours, which is in a pure and elevated style of art. Those imbeciles have selected figures suitable for statuary.

I know that any words I could say would be powerless to console you, and that you must be almost on the brink of despair.

When one misses an opportunity one is apt to fancy that another will never present itself. And the more one thinks about the disappointment the more enraged one becomes. Afterward one recovers one's serenity and makes up for what one has missed, for one can do this with a determined will. This is what one must be well persuaded of. Weak natures bewail the past; those who have energy and intelligence make the future avenge the past. These are not idle words, they are the truth.

Throw your chagrin out of the door of the railway carriage and do not look back. And then they will have to begin over again. They cannot afflict Paris with the D—— column, or the F—— cubes. It will be I who shall get the work and in return you will make a monument for me when I am dead.

Meantime, amuse yourself; bring back your painter restored to health, and all will go well. Paint hard and at the coming Salon, we shall all three triumph.

I can no longer make a likeness.[1]

---

[1] See the letter reproduced in fac-simile.

Je pourrais vous retourner votre : ce sont des âmes sœurs.

Ce qui est certain, c'est que les projets admis sont inférieurs au vôtre qui est d'un art très-pur et très-idéal. Les imbéciles ont choisi des figures de sculpteurs.

Je sais bien que tout ce qu'on peut dire là-dessus n'est pas une consolation, et vous devez être bien près de penser que si

la fin de tout.
Tantôt en pleine occasion on s'imagine qu'il ne s'en trouvera plus jamais d'autre. Et plus on réfléchit, plus c'est enrageant. Puis on se calme, puis on se rattrape, car on se rattrape absolument avec de la volonté. C'est ce qu'il faut bien se mettre dans la tête. Les faibles pensent au passé, les forts et les intelligents prennent leur revanche. Ce ne sont pas des phrases c'est la vérité.

Maxim Gorki

Fermez votre magasin par les portières des wagons et ne regardez pas en arrière. Du reste ils seront obligés de recommencer. Impossible d'affliger Paris de la colonne... ou des cubes. !

C'est moi qui l'ai voulu. Et en vérité vous ferez mon monument quand je serai morte.

En attendant, promenez-vous, ramenez votre peintre guéri et tout ira bien. Faites de la peinture et ne marchandez. Salam

nous triompherions
tous les trois.

1ʳᵉ Médaille
x x
N.B. Parceque je
suis modeste.

Médaille
d'Honneur

Médaille
de 2ᵉ classe pour
un paysage.

Je ne sais plus faire
la ressemblance.

Marie Bashkirtseff

To M. E——.

30 Rue Ampère, Paris, May.

Dear Monsieur:

As the arrangements for your concert will be attended with considerable expense, permit me to advance you the inclosed trifle, on account, for the tickets which I shall dispose of. But do not, I beg of you, regard this little service as a favor. You will oblige me by saying nothing about it to mamma. Your speaking of it would only make me look foolish, as if I were doing a kindness, when, in reality, this is a very usual thing among artists. And I have just sold a little study. It is understood, then, that you are to say nothing about the matter; otherwise you will displease me seriously.

To M. de M——.

Monsieur:

I read your works, I might almost say, with delight. In truth to nature, which you copy with religious fidelity, you find an inspiration that is truly sublime, while you move your readers by touches of feeling so profoundly human, that we fancy we see ourselves depicted in your pages, and love you with an egotistical love. Is this an unmeaning compliment? Be indulgent, it is sincere in the main.

You will understand that I should like to say many fine and striking things to you, but it is rather difficult, all at once, in this way. I regret this all the more as you are sufficiently great to inspire one with romantic dreams of becoming the confidant of your beautiful soul, always supposing your soul to be beautiful.

If your soul is not beautiful, and if "those things are not in your line," I shall regret it for your sake, in the first place; and in the next I shall set you down in my mind as a maker of literature, and dismiss the matter from my thoughts.

For a year past I have had the wish to write to you and was many times on the point of doing so, but—sometimes I thought I exaggerated your merits and that it was not worth while. Two days ago, however, I saw suddenly, in the *Gaulois*, that some one had honored you with a flattering epistle and that you had inquired the address of this amiable person in order to answer him. I at once became jealous, your literary merits dazzled me anew and—here is my letter.

And now let me say that I shall always preserve my incognito for you. I do not even desire to see you from a distance—your countenance might not please me—who can tell? All I know of you now is that you are young and that you are not married, two essential points, even for a distant adoration.

But I must tell you that I am charming; this sweet reflection will stimulate you to answer my letter. It seems to me that if I were a man I should wish to hold no communication, not even an epistolary one, with an old fright of an Englishwoman, whatever might be thought by

    Miss Hastings,
    P. O. Station of the Madeleine.

To the Same.

Your letter, Monsieur, did not at all surprise me, and I did not by any means expect what you seem to think.

But let me first say that I did not ask to be your confidant—that would be a little too foolish; and if you have the time to re-read my letter, you will see what you might have seen at a glance had you deigned to take notice of it—the ironical and disparaging manner in which I speak of myself.

You mention to me also the sex of your other correspondent; I thank you for reassuring me on that point, but as my jealousy was of an altogether spiritual nature, it is a matter of little consequence to me.

To answer me by giving me your confidence—this would be the act of an imbecile, considering that you do not know me. Would it be to take advantage of your sensibility, Monsieur, to recall to your mind, as a settler, the death of Henry IV? To answer me by giving me your confidence, since you thought that I asked it from you by return of post, would have been to amuse yourself wittily at my expense; and if I had been in your place I should have done so, for I am sometimes merry enough—although I am often sad too—to dream of exchanging confidences by letter with an unknown philosopher, and sharing his impressions of the carnival. That description, two columns long, was altogether satisfactory, and very graphic. I read it over three times, but in exchange, what an old story, that of the old mother who avenges herself on the Prussians! (That must have occurred about the time you were reading my letter.)

As for the charm conferred by mystery, everything depends upon taste. That it does not amuse you—very good; but that it amuses me intensely I confess in all sincerity, as I do the infantile delight given me by your letter, such as it was.

And then, if that sort of thing does not amuse you, it is because not one of your sixty correspondents has been able to awaken an interest in you—that is all, and if I have not been able to strike the right chord, either, I am too reasonable to bear you any ill will on that account.

Only sixty? I should have supposed you besieged by a greater number. Have you answered them all?

Perhaps my mental qualities do not suit you—in which case you would be hard to please; in short, I imagine that I know you (this, too, is the effect novelists produce on weak-headed women of the middle classes). It may be that you are right, however.

As I write to you with the utmost frankness, in consequence of the feeling I have mentioned, you think me, perhaps, a sentimental young person, or even an adventuress. This would be very vexatious. Make no excuses, therefore, for your want of romance, of gallantry, etc.

Decidedly my letter must have been stupid.

To my great regret, then, it seems we must remain as we are—unless I should take the notion some day to prove to you that I do not deserve to be number 61. As for your reasoning, it is sound; but you are mistaken in the facts. I forgive you for it, then, and even for the erasures, and the old woman, and the Prussians!

May you be happy!

However, if you need only a vague description to induce you to disclose to me the beauties of your withered and scentless soul, take this: Fair hair, medium height, born sometime between 1812 and 1863. And intellectually!—no, I should seem a braggart and you would know at once that I was from Marseilles.

P. S.—Excuse the blots, erasures, etc.

But I have already copied my letter three times!

To the Same.

You are horribly bored!

Ah, cruel one! You say this in order to leave me no illusion regarding the cause of your favor of—which for the rest arrived very opportunely and delighted me.

It is true that I am only amusing myself, but it is not true that I am as well acquainted with you as you say. I assure you solemnly that I do not even know the color of your complexion or your height, and of your private character I know only as much as I gather from the lines you favor me with, and that through the disguise of not a little evil-mindedness and affectation.

In short, for a dull naturalist, you are not stupid, and my answer would be a volume if I did not restrain myself through vanity. I must not let you think that all my energy goes in that direction.

Let us settle accounts about the old stories, in the first place, if you will; that will take some time, for do you know that you overwhelm me with them? You are right—in the main.

But art consists precisely in making us admire old stories, charming us with them eternally, as Nature charms with her eternal sun, her ancient earth, and her men built all on the same pattern, and all animated by the same feelings; but—there are also musicians who have only a few notes, and painters who have only a few colors. And then, you know as well as I do that you wish to make me pose. Why, then, I am only too highly honored.

Old stories, let it be!—the mother in the power of the Prussians in literature, and Jeanne d'Arc in painting.

Are you in truth sure that a *wit* (is that the word) would not find in them a new and touching side?

As a weekly chronicle, indeed, your letter is well enough, and what I say of it—and those other old stories about your profession being a hard one! You take me for a *bourgeoise* who takes you for a poet, and you endeavor to enlighten me. George Sand boasted of writing for money, and the industrious Flaubert bewailed his poverty.

The suffering he makes others feel he felt himself. Balzac made no such complaint but was always full of enthusiasm for his work. As for Montesquieu, if I may venture to express an opinion, his taste for study was so keen that, as it was the source of his fame, it was also the source of his happiness, as the undermistress of your imaginary school would say.

As far as being well paid is concerned, it is all very well, for no one was ever really famous without being also rich, as the Jew Baahrou, the contemporary of Job, says. (Fragments preserved by the learned Spitzbube, of Berlin.) And then, everything gains by a good setting—beauty, genius, even religion. Did not God come himself to give directions to his servant Moses concerning the ornaments of the tabernacle, explaining to him that the cherubim on either side should be of gold, and of *exquisite workmanship*.

So then, you are bored, and you look upon everything with indifference, and you have not a spark of poetry in your soul? Do you think in this way to frighten me? I fancy I can see you now; you have a rotund figure, you wear a waistcoat of an undecided color, too short for you, and with the last button unfastened. Well, even so, you interest me. What I cannot understand is how you should be bored. I myself am sometimes sad, discouraged, enraged, but bored—never!

You are not the man I am in search of?

I am in search of no one, Monsieur,

and I think that, for a strong-minded woman (the dried up old maid), men should be only accessories.

The dried-up old maid—misery! there she comes—the *concierge*. "Would you be so kind as to tell me how this is done?"

At last I am going to answer your questions, and with perfect frankness, for I do not like to take advantage of the simplicity of a man of genius who goes to sleep after dinner smoking his cigar.

Am I slender? Oh, no; but neither am I stout. Worldly, sentimental, romantic? But what meaning do you attach to those words? It seems to me that there is room for them all in one and the same person, everything depends on the time, the occasion, the circumstances. I am an *opportuniste*, and peculiarly susceptible to moral contagion; therefore I may in time become as unromantic as you are. What perfume do I use?—Virtue. Vulgo, none.

Yes, I am a *gourmande;* or rather, I have a fastidious appetite. I have small ears, not very well shaped, but pretty; my eyes are gray. Yes, I am a musician, but probably not so good a pianist as your under-school-mistress.

Are you satisfied with my docility? If so, unfasten another button of your waistcoat and think of me when the twilight shades are falling. If not—so much the worse; I think I have given you a great deal in exchange for your pretended confidences.

May I venture to ask you which are your favorite musicians and painters?

And how if I were a man?[1]

To the Same.

I am now going to tell you something which may seem incredible, which you, especially, will never believe and which, coming after the event, has only a historical value. It is that I, too, have had enough of it. At your third letter my enthusiasm was cooled. Satiety?——

And then, I prize only that which I am not sure of. I should, then, now come to you.

[1] To this letter is appended a sketch representing a stout man sitting asleep in an easy chair, under the shade of a palm tree on the seashore; beside him is a table on which are a glass of beer and a cigar.

Why did I first write to you? I awoke one fine morning and found that I was a wonderful being surrounded by fools. It grieved me to see the precious pearls of my genius thrown before swine——

What if I were to write to some famous man, a man worthy of comprehending me? That would be charming, romantic, and—who could tell?—after a certain number of letters I should perhaps, in this novel way, have acquired a friend. Then I asked myself who this man should be, and I selected you!

Such a correspondence could be possible only under two conditions.

The second of these is an *unbounded* admiration on the part of the unknown. From an *unbounded* admiration arises a bond of sympathy which causes one to express one's self in such a way as will inevitably touch and interest the famous man.

Neither of these conditions exists here. I chose you with the hope of conceiving for you, later on, an unbounded admiration! For I then thought you comparatively young. I began, then, with feigning admiration for you, and I have ended by saying "unbecoming" and even rude things to you, admitting what you have condescended to perceive. At the point at which we have arrived, I may confess that your odious letter has made me pass a very bad day.

I feel as deeply wounded as if I had received a real offense, which is absurd.

Adieu, with pleasure.

If you still keep them, send me my autographs; as for yours, I have already sold them in America at a ridiculous price.

To the Same.

I understand your distrust. It is very unlikely that a woman *comme il faut*, who is both young and pretty, should amuse herself writing to you. Is that it? But, Monsieur—but I was going to forget that all is over between us. I think you deceive yourself. And it is very good of me to tell you so, for it will make me cease to be interesting to you, if I have ever been so. You shall see how I put myself in your place. An unknown appears upon the horizon; if the adventure is easy, it has no attraction for me; if *impossible*, it would be useless, and a bore to attempt it.

I have not the happiness to be between these two extremes, and I tell you so good-naturedly, since we have made up.

What I find very amusing is, that while I am telling you the simple truth you imagine that I am trying to mystify you.

I do not go into republican society, although I am a red republican?

No, because I do not wish to meet you.

And you, do you not, then, desire a little romance in the midst of your Parisian materialism? A spiritual friendship? I do not refuse to meet you, and I am even going to make arrangements for doing so without giving you notice. If you knew that you were being observed for a purpose it might make you look foolish. This must be avoided. Your terrestrial envelope is indifferent to me, it is true; but is mine so to you? Let us suppose that you should have the bad taste not to find me a wonderful being, do you think I should be satisfied, however innocent my intentions? I do not say but that some day—I even count upon surprising you not a little on that day.

Meantime, if it bores you, let us not write to each other any more. I reserve to myself the right, however, of writing to you, when any atrocity comes into my head.

You distrust me; that is very natural.

Well, then, I am going to give you such a means as a woman of the people might give you of convincing yourself that I am not a woman of the people.

Only do not laugh.

Go to a clairvoyant, and let him sense my letter, and he will tell you my age, the color of my hair, my surroundings, etc.

You will write to let me know what he has revealed to you.

"Humbug, stupidity, nonsense," you will say.

Ah! Monsieur, that is perfectly true; even I do not deny it. But in my case it is because I desire great things which I have not attained—yet. And with you the same must be the case.

I am not so simple as to ask you what are your secret aspirations, although my illness has revived in me a candor *à la* Chérie.

How *naïf* is that old Japanese naturalist in a Louis XV wig!

And you think that after writing, nothing would be simpler than to come and say, "I am he."

I assure you, that that would annoy me exceedingly.

They say you admire only strong-minded women with black hair.

Is that true?

To see each other! Let me then, charm you by my——literature, you who have had such success in that line!

To the Same.

In writing to you again I ruin myself forever in your estimation. But that is a matter of indifference to me, and then, I do it only to avenge myself—oh, only by telling you the result of your ruse to discover what my disposition was.

I was positively afraid to send to the post-office, imagining a thousand absurd things. *This man* will probably end our correspondence by—consideration for your modesty forbids me to proceed. And as I opened the envelope I prepared myself for anything, so as not to be surprised.

I was surprised, however, but agreeably so.

> Devant les doux accents d'un noble repentir
> Me faut-il donc, seigneur, cesser de vous haïr?

Unless, indeed, this be another ruse. Flattered at being taken for a woman of the world she will try to act the character after drawing forth a human document that I am very well pleased to be able to explain in this way.

Then why was I displeased? This is perhaps not a conclusive proof that I was so, dear Monsieur. In fine, adieu. I forgive you, if you care for my forgiveness, because I am ill, and as that is a rare thing with me, I am full of compassion for myself, for every one, for you! who have found the means of making yourself so extremely—disagreeable to me. I take the less trouble to deny the accusation, as you will in any case believe what you choose in the matter.

How shall I prove to you that

neither am I playing a part, nor am I your enemy?

And to what end should I try to do so?

It would be equally impossible to try to convince you that we are made to understand each other. You are not my equal. I am sorry for it. Nothing would give me greater pleasure than to be able to acknowledge your superiority—or that of any one else.

I should like to have some one to talk to. Your last article was interesting, and I even wished, apropos of girls, to put a plain question to you.

But——

.   .   .   .   .

An innocent remark in your letter,

however, has given me food for thought.

It distresses you to have given me pain. This is either very silly or very charming. You may ridicule me, but that will only make me laugh. Yes, it was a slight attack of romanticism you had—*à la* Stendhal, nothing more; but make your mind easy, you will not die of it this time.

Good-night.

To Baron de Saint-Amand.

30 RUE AMPÈRE, April.

My Dear Friend:

Ah! how I should like to have a *salon* where literature and society should both be represented—an interesting *salon*. That would be to enjoy life and to work at the same time.

The days follow one another, time flies, life is passing away.

And a moderate amount of success would not compensate me for what I have suffered; for this a dazzling success, a triumph would be necessary—a revenge on fate.

The truth is that I have always experienced, and that I experience more and more every day, an imperious necessity to write. I invent stories, I see real and imaginary events. Dumas says that the dominating faculty of woman is intuition. Well, by intuition I comprehend, I see, I know extraordinary things, but when I find myself in the midst of my papers—for I have a large portfolio full of notes——

When I write, my glance falls on the fingers of my left hand; those living, nervous fingers make me think of Jules Bastien-Lepage's painting; the hands he paints are so life-like; the skin is real, the muscles look as if they were going to move.

You know that I go every day to Sèvres. My picture has taken complete possession of me—the young girl sitting in a revery, at the foot of the apple-tree, "languid and intoxicated," as André Theuriet says, by the balmy air. If I succeed in rendering the effect of the budding life of spring, of the sunshine, it will be beautiful.

Good-by for a while.

To her Brother.

Rue Ampère, Paris,
Friday, May 30.

Dear Paul:

Mme. Z—— is a queer little woman; her husband is a senator, besides being a *savant*, a litterateur, a man of ability, who has translated the masterpieces of the Russian language, and worn mourning for Gambetta. On the occasion of her first visit to Paris she went to see "Severo Torelli," a drama of François Coppée, at the Odéon. Enchanted by it, she went to the doorkeeper of the theater to ask for the author's address, in order to express her admiration to him.

This was what is not to be seen in France—genuine enthusiasm expressing itself frankly, without fear of ridicule.

She then wrote to Coppée, obtained an interview, wrote to him again from Rome, and brought him from there a picture, a copy of a Madonna. The poet wrote to her thanking her for the picture and expressing his regret at being unable to do so personally, his time not being at his own disposal. Mme. Z—— was not discouraged, and it never occurred to her that she might be boring him. *She charged* me to write a dispatch to Coppée, as follows :

Monsieur :

I remain here until Saturday, and I have been forced by four enthusiastic young girls to promise them that they shall see François Coppée. However accustomed you may be to receiving homage, you cannot refuse that of these youthful admirers, which has at least the merit of being sincere. Tell us then when we may expect you.

Z. Z.

Yesterday we received the answer of François Coppée, of the French Academy, saying that he would have the honor of presenting himself at Mme. Z——'s, on Friday, at half-past one, or two at the furthest.

And at 2 o'clock he was there in our drawing-room, with mamma, Mme. Z——, Mlle. S——, Mme. Z——'s niece, Dina, and myself.

You know that I am very self-possessed, but I was one of the four enthusiastic young girls; although he must have observed that I did not look so silly as the others. The Canroberts have dined with him at the Princess Mathilde's; he had conversed with Claire, and I spoke to him of her.

He seated himself in an arm-chair, drank some tea, and smoked. The tea-table was brought in with the tea already served, as on the stage, and at one time we were all six watching him at once, as he drank his tea. He noticed it, and the great poet carried his amiability so far as to ask to see my studio, and to request me, when he was taking his leave, to send him word when I should have a new picture to show.

He is very agreeable, but his appearance is somewhat remarkable. I am very glad to know him. He has blue eyes, and he looked at me steadily as he spoke, as if he wished to discover what my thoughts were.

In short, this Parisian must have been

very much embarrassed by the serious admiration of which he found himself the object. Good-by.

To M. Henry Houssaye, of the Revue des Deux Mondes.

Monsieur:

Foreigners are like the great Molière; they take what suits them, wherever they find it. If we had been imitators, this might serve as our excuse. What is surprising is that an art critic of your merit should say that one copies such or such a painter by such or such a system; that one employs such or such a process, because one does not settle down forever in a specialty dear to the dealers.

Neither M. Bastien-Lepage nor the

troop of foreigners whom you mention dream, I think, of following or adjuring Japanese, or primitive, or any other style of art. They copy what they see with sincerity, without artifice, with more or less ability. If they find their subject in the street, they work in the street; if in a studio, they work in the studio. You are too observant not to have noticed the differences in the various kinds of light. To paint sailors on the seashore, in the open air, where the light is difficult to manage, or *gamins* at the street corner where one sees them, is this to follow a system?

Be just. If a painter were to give an interior the same atmosphere as an out-of-doors scene, that would be a system, conventional treatment. We have not done this. We have painted our subjects as we have seen them, to the best of our ability. Excuse these few remarks and do not slander us.

ONE OF THE FOREIGN PAINTERS MENTIONED.

To M. Edmond de Goncourt.

Monsieur:

Like all the rest of the world I have read " Chérie," and, between ourselves, the book is full of poor passages. She who has the boldness to write to you now is a young girl who was brought up among luxurious, fashionable, at times peculiar surroundings. This young girl, who three months ago, completed her twenty-third year, is well-educated, an artist, and ambitious.

She has several note-books, which contain her impressions as she has recorded them, from the time she was twelve years old. She has concealed nothing. The young girl in question is, besides, endowed with a feeling of pride, which has obliged her in these notes to set herself down exactly as she is.

To show these records to any one would be to lay bare to him her inmost soul. But she has a love for all true art—excessive, insensate, if you will. She thinks it would interest you to see this journal. You have said somewhere that you read with delight the record of any real experience. Well, she who has accomplished nothing as yet, but who has the vanity to think she already comprehends the sentiments of men of genius, shares your feeling, and at the risk of appearing in your eyes a madwoman or an impostor, offers you her journal. Only you will understand, Monsieur, the necessity of observing *absolute* secrecy in the matter. The young girl resides in Paris, goes into society, and the people whom she mentions are all living. This letter is addressed to a great writer, to an artist, to a *savant*, and consequently requires no excuse, in my opinion. But by most people, by those around me, I should be looked upon as either insane or reprobate if they were to know what I have written to you.

I at one time wished to form an epistolary friendship with some young writer of genius, with the object of bequeathing to him my journal (at that time it was thought that I had not long to live). I prefer to give it to you during my lifetime.

If you think that what I desire is your autograph, you need not sign what you do me the honor to write to me.

J. R. I. (*poste restante*).

To M. Emile Zola.

Monsieur:

I have read all that you have ever written, without missing a single word. If you have ever so slight a consciousness of your own merits, you will understand my enthusiasm. And in order that you may not think this enthusiasm mere silly gush, I will say that I am very exacting and very critical in the matter of literature, having read almost everything, in addition to having studied the classics, although I am a woman.

You are a great *savant* and a great artist, but the quality in you which more particularly excites my admiration is your love for Truth. I have the audacity to share it. Is it not audacity to say I share anything with a great genius like you?

I know well that you are above being flattered by the admiration of anonymous correspondents, you cannot be pleased by the wretched homage of "a woman who approaches you, etc." But the feeling that forces me to write to you is irresistible, and if I only knew how to express myself you would be touched by it.

I could wish you to be alone and in need of pity. Here is a very feminine, a very romantic, and a very commonplace sentiment, which I fancy I feel differently from others. Do not think that I am overflowing with ridiculous sensibility. I am not an adventuress, nor even a woman to whom adventures would be possible, although I am young. But I confess that I am foolish enough to have cherished the impossible dream of an epistolary friendship with you, and if you knew what a formidable being you are in my eyes you would laugh at my courage.

I do not suppose that you will answer me. They say you are in private life a complete *bourgeois*.

That would give me pain, but accept, in any case, Monsieur, the homage of the most profound, the truest, and the sincerest admiration.

To M——.

Can it be possible that in all Paris, among the thousands of journals which abound here, there is not one to be found in which a man who belongs to no party, or in which men belonging to different parties may freely express an opinion, may defend or attack this or that man or idea without therefor committing themselves to some political clique, and submitting to be labelled and classified according to a system which forces on them certain obligations and reticences—an independent journal, in short, a journal without *party prejudices.* Alas! they almost all declare they have no party prejudices and they are all alike illiberal *routiniers* and prejudiced.

Where is the republican journal that would do justice to an original idea of a churchman? They would say that those people have no ideas. But let us suppose them to have such ideas.

Where is the reactionary journal, whose columns are not constantly filled with stupid, pointless, and tiresome attacks on the Republic?

There are so-called ministerial journals, which either approve unreservedly or maintain silence when they should censure. Such journals are wanting in patriotism.

There is the radical journal, which holds the wildest political views, but which has on its side the diabolical wit of M. de Rochefort.

There are clerico-Bonapartist journals, journals devoted to cabbage culture and to vine culture, but an independent journal in which any one may express his idea, provided only it be a good one, or plead his cause, provided he do so with ability, there is none!

You hate the folly of people who will have a master at any cost, and you say that it needs the soul of a valet to love a monarchy. You are a republican. Very good. What then?

Under pain of forfeiture you are compelled to disapprove of everything that those of any other party say or do.

Do you approve an act of the government? You are bought by the ministers!

Do you speak in eulogistic terms of Gambetta? You are an *opportuniste*, then, a sorry creature, an imbecile who does not understand a word about the matter. The *opportuniste* is a man who does everything with a purpose. Could there be anything more sensible? But you hate, that is to say, you envy Gambetta; and in your eyes an *opportuniste* is a man who has all the evil tendencies you choose to attribute to him.

Discover justice in a demand *à la* Ruggieri, of M. Rochefort, and you are attacked as a leveler, a radical. This is another excellent word, whose meaning, like that of the word *opportuniste*, has been distorted. Who is there who is not a radical when he ardently desires to accomplish any purpose.

Then there is no way in which one can be an honest citizen and express one's self freely in regard to public events, giving one's views concerning them without first thinking of what spectacles he must put on to observe them through? It seems not.

Suppose a writer has given utterance to republican sentiments and afterward allows himself to be just to— Prince Napoleon, let us say; to find that he has wit or genius. It will immediately be asked:

"By whom is he paid?"

Is it not a maneuver to discredit X——, to attach him, in spite of himself, to the party of Z——?

Sad, sad.

The journal you sigh for is a journal of amateurs, then? Precisely! Amateurs of liberty. A journal that would be capable of defending the capacity of M. Jules Simon or of Prince Napoleon, the talent of Gambetta or the wit of Rochefort, or of bearing witness to the weakness of M. Clemenceau. A journal which should flatter no passion, in short. But that is not possible, they say; for if you find amateurs to write you will find none to read, and from our earliest infancy the words *read* and *write* have been inseparably associated in our minds.

Ah, bah! Is there not, then, to be found in France a handful of people who, like us, are disgusted with party prejudice; who say to themselves, like us, that there is only one France, one party, and that every man useful to the state should be employed; that all talent should be protected, all waste stopped? What! is there not a handful of men to be found who, scorning the stupid accusations that may be brought against them, will be content to proclaim themselves honestly proud of their country's glory and ready to support men of talent in whatever rank they may be classed by the amateurs in ticketing, and equally ready to censure whatever seems to them reprehensible, however exalted its source?

An ideal journal where one could say, for instance, that one loved the Republic and admired Gambetta, but in which one could also express one's surprise that so eminent a man should allow such a piece of folly as the expulsion of the Jesuits to be committed. The Jesuits and other religious orders are dangerous—well, then, get rid of them! It is your place to find the means of doing so—you are the government, you are our intelligence. M. Gambetta allows follies to be perpetrated, to prove, perhaps, that he is not all-powerful. And where is the harm of being thought so, as M. Ranc has said?

A journal in which one could express one's surprise at the injustice done to the eminent qualities of Prince Napoleon, without being suspected of being in the pay of Plon-Plon; one's contempt of the Bonapartist party and one's regret that the before-mentioned citizen should be surrounded by men who discredit, while thinking they serve him. The only good statesmanship is that which succeeds, they say. Succeeds in what?

Let the citizen Jérôme go into business or rid him by a miracle of the compromising and compromised name he bears, for otherwise how could you expect him to succeed. Whatever the Bonapartist party may be now, before the death of the young prince he sometimes received the popular suffrages; now this is not the case.

Go explain to the electors the intentions of the prince, those, at least, which he proclaims, and he will again receive their suffrages, but not in the way you wish. Either he is very deceitful or he is excessively liberal as well as highly intelligent. He should not believe in his rights. If he does, we retract all we have said.

Explain Prince Napoleon's intentions to the electors! We shall take good care not to do so. The policy of Napoleon III must be carried out. Ah! And the attitude of the prince on the night of the *coup d'état ;* and his political views, are they so opposed to those of his cousin? Ingratitude— a fine word, and what an effect it produces! We are far, alas, from the severity of morals of the ancient Romans, and where is the brother or the cousin who does not profit, be it ever so slightly, by the position of his relation? Perhaps the prince will not be pleased to be defended by us. For we frankly throw overboard both his rights and the Bonapartist party—that party which says: Let him be what he will so that he be successful. Ah, wretches!

And progress, and patriotism, and honesty—are these not to be taken into account? Here is a man who has places at his disposal. Their convictions are social prejudices and the hope of recovering a lost position. The most prominent, the *strongest* of them will tell you seriously that their habits, their education, forbid them to associate with people who do not wash their hands. Innocent excuse! As if it had not been long since proved that the clergy are those who wash themselves least and that the unfortunate children in the convents are given a bath once a month, and then in the dark.

But we have said a great deal about M. Jérôme Bonaparte.

Ah, then, so much the worse. It is a logical beginning.

Who will doubt of our independence, seeing us making a quasi-eulogy of the most unpopular man in France—unless they accuse us of being subsidized by him !

Horrible social chaos !

To M. Tony Robert-Fleury.

30 RUE AMPÈRE, PARIS.

Monsieur:

I have just learned with surprise that the chagrin I felt in the matter of the *Salon* medal has been misconstrued by you into a feeling of animosity on my part toward yourself. And as it is chiefly to you that I owe my artistic education, I do not wish to let such a misconception remain in your mind an instant longer than I can help. I make no apology, as I have none to make, but I greatly desire that my words, my complaints, and my indignation, which I persist in thinking justifiable, may not be misinterpreted.

I am perfectly conscious of all that has been done for me; you, alone, could do no more; you see, then, that I am not very unreasonable.

Accept, my dear master, the expression of my highest consideration.

To M. Sully-Prudhomme.

JUNE.

Monsieur:

I have just read, and understood, as I think, "Lucrèce," and the "Preface" to it. Do not thank me for this, although without being either old or ugly, I have read, in addition to your "Lucrèce," all that you have ever written. Repay me now in kind. What I write will be neither so fine nor so voluminous.

And indeed I am at a loss what to say; frightened at my audacity (an embryo blue-stocking), naturally I cannot succeed in expressing myself as I wish. You are of too serious a disposition to attach any value to letters from an unknown correspondent; you are forty years of age, you have many old friends—what would you do with a new adorer? And yet I have cherished the hope, a very *naïve* one, probably, and worthy of the days of 1830, of gaining your friendship through a correspondence with you.

I might content myself with making your personal acquaintance, but then I could only say commonplaces to you.

While under my incognito I can frankly tell you that I have the daring and the presumption to understand and to share your most delicate thoughts, which I could not say to you *viva voce*. And, in general, poetry produces no effect upon me except when it is bad; then it makes me impatient. If it pleases people to rhyme, let them rhyme, so long as I am not obliged to read their verses.

I understood the work, but I found it necessary, in order to do so, to concentrate my thoughts. It is in vain that I tell myself that the management of ideas is familiar to you and that I am very silly to admire your skill in the expression and arrangement of your thoughts.

For you, on your side, must also admire the skill of the painter who manipulates his colors and makes with them, by means of combinations which you do not understand, varied and beautiful pictures. But doubtless you think your work of rummaging *uselessly* among the secret chambers of human thought far superior to the work of the painter.

To the Same.

Ah! Monsieur:

I am indeed filled with profound esteem for you, the more so as I found it harder to understand your preface to "Lucrèce" than the work itself. It is infinitely more difficult to understand than the philosophy of the ancients, and I have so high an opinion of my own intelligence that any one who succeeds in puzzling me becomes in my eyes a giant. This is the case with you. I had read all your works, with the exception of "Lucrèce," and seeing you manage these abstruse subjects so easily, I experience a veneration akin to worship for you.

To M. Julian.

Dear Master:

I see that you wish to take the place of M⸻. Your letter is very pretty but, as usual, you attribute meannesses to me which you believe on the authority of the gossips of the studio. I have never insulted any one there. I have too much delicacy of feeling to do so consciously. And I am not sufficiently stupid to do so unconsciously. One must be base to wish to humiliate an inferior. As to the remarks about carriages, dinners, etc., no one who has ever known me could suppose me capable of making them.

I have said that you attribute meannesses to me, but as my conscience is clear I am not affected by your doing so. It would be a waste of time to try to convince people. As to my talent, I hold it in high esteem, and not even in my dreams would I compare myself to your *protégé*. Few painters have notices like those which I have received this year. I have, besides, just sold two studies, one to an amateur and one to a dealer, both of them strangers to me.

It is easily seen that I must have

provoked you to make you say things you cannot believe. If I wrote to you to retract what I said, it was under the influence of T. R. F., who says that you had been very friendly toward me. And also because I have reflected that, after all, to prefer the ridiculous X—— to me is to me no injury. You are free to do so, only it is amusing, that is all.

And then, you and I can never quarrel; it is altogether impossible. Although you may pretend to think ill of me in order to tease me, you know very well in your heart that I am the truest, the most admirable, the most just, the greatest, and the most loyal creature in the world. I speak seriously. You know I care nothing for those who do not understand me; those whom I do care for, understand me. And then I am on the eve of obtaining a European reputation. *Quarrel with so admirable and wonderful a being?* How absurd!

I cannot better reply to your witty letter than by eulogizing myself, a eulogy deduced from and based upon a profound knowledge of myself, of this wonderful and unique *me*, who fills me with delight, and whom, like Narcissus, I adore! Find me in all Paris, if you can, any one who could write such a composition at a stroke. Doubtless, if you compare my talent as a painter to my talent as a pamphleteer and polemist—

APPENDIX.

My dear children, Alexis and Bojidar:

Do not weep with joy when your eyes fall on these characters traced by my own hand.

I want to know what your plans are—that is to say, those of Alexis, for at present he is the model I dream of for my picture, which I have begun to paint in a garden filled with the most luscious fruits; seriously, it is at Passy, and is charming; the railroad passes close by; it is an ideal garden. Let Alexis then, the Alexis of my picture, inform me without delay if I can count upon him for a couple of sittings during the present month. In September, as you know, my twenty-nine gowns will take me to Biarritz. But I foresee that you will soon return. Julian needs Bojidar and I need Alexis, without whom the picture would run a very poor chance of being finished. Good-by, dear and venerated co-religionists. Do not slight my request.

ANDREY.

P. S.—If the sea air has not turned you into salt, answer quickly, giving your *common* consent, but in a *distingué* style.

Illustrious Pupil:

Your papa St. Amand will give you this letter. Be very obedient and take this great man's advice in everything.

You have dared to remain eight days without letting Circe hear from you, which makes me think that she has already transformed you into a—I will not say what. You do not deserve, then, that I should cast before you the pearls of my genius. Think of her and of them. You will never be anything unless you respect the great artists.

Good-night.

Dear Bojidar:

M. S—— has gone away, leaving his affairs in great disorder, and even those who regard him with the most indulgence do not hesitate to speak very seriously about the matter. Among other stories there is one about a duel on account of a blow given by

S——, at Monaco. He has simply fled, after having been publicly branded as a coward by Tarderet and Mestayer. Barnola was unlucky in having given him lodgings. In short, do not go to see him in Paris; it is to tell you this that I write to you now.

I cannot get that crazy Bernhardt out of my mind, and the more I think of her, the more I think that when she committed that piece of idiotic folly she must have been raving mad.

Good-by.

ANDREY.

Have you seen M. Julian?

I don't know to what letter of About's you have reference, O Couvelet! Notwithstanding the disrespectful way in which you treat Mother Joseph, I want to tell you that we were present at the grand civic review at Longchamps by Martineux and his ministers. Although the spectators (who were not very numerous) were closely packed together, the authorities were able to regain their equipages without difficulty, thanks to Joseph, who was intrusted with the duty of calling the state coaches. You were not mistaken, O Couvelet! you uttered a great truth; Joseph was really put in charge of the cloak-room, with ten attendants under his orders. In addition to this the poor angel was obliged to accompany an usher who carried around glasses of champagne, and to carry around himself a white plate full of *madeleines*. Alas! Jean is severe with his courtiers. When the review was over, Antinous-Joseph was panting for breath—he had run about so much—and Mother Joseph Couvelet herself took him into her carriage and drove him home. I hasten to explain the matter to you, for I take it for granted, O Father Couvelet! that you are as jealous of Mother Couvelet as Mother Joseph is of Joseph.

Just as I was about to close this letter I learned—O horror! that Joseph dined yesterday in a restaurant *au gros-caillou*, and was afterward picked up from the sidewalk in front of the Morgue.

Dear Bojidar:

Will you come with us to skate to-morrow at three o'clock? Ask your brother to come also. And afterward I will make a visit to your mother, and after that the whole party will dine with us.

MARIE BASHKIRTSEFF.

Horrible Bojidar:

I received your letter on my return from Passy, where I remained a fortnight. I am very glad to see that you still venerate truly great men. Beware of angling. The other day they took a poor madman to Charenton, who angled from his stall in the balcony for a *première*. They say he is a sculptor. I have not seen either of the two brothers for a long time. It is said that the elder brother is going to St. Petersburg to paint the columns of the Cathedral of St. Isaac. (They are of malachite and consequently green.) He is also commissioned by the government to dye 1,000,000 yards of ribbon for the new decoration of the order of agricultural excellence.

. . . .

Write to me soon, and beware of angling and of sculpture; they lead in the end to madness.

I write you a line in haste as I have just learned that you have been presented to the baroness; she is all-powerful at the Théâtre Italien. Be amiable and adroit, and manage to procure us a box.

If you do this, I will invite you to dine with us when G—— does. He dined here yesterday with his brother, Émile. They have a great regard for you, notwithstanding all the evil things I say of you. Be sure and arrange about the box, and write to me immediately.

Success to angling!

MARIE BASHKIRTSEFF.

A great many remembrances to Agathe.

Illustrious friend of Sarah:

If you do not take the trip, so much the better for the dogs and so much the worse for you. I will hasten my return, for I am distressed to think of the trouble Prater must give you. If, however, by some extraordinary chance we should not be home at the time of the removal of the provisions from 37, arrange about the aforesaid removal ; all the treasures of the canteen are to be transferred to the apartment of Mlle. Oelnitz—the last one to the right, opening on the court. The precious paintings and the sumptuous tapestries, likewise. I should be ashamed to trouble you with so many things if I did not know that I would do as much for you with pleasure. Put the twenty francs you mention into the savings bank for me; that will be a little nest-egg against my return, and then I will be able to lend you some of the cash. Many remembrances to Julian, if he has returned; tell him that I have met Diaz de Soria and that perhaps I will paint his portrait at Madrid; that is to say, a sketch only, which I will show to him before painting it. Has Tony returned? Good-by. Direct your letters to Biarritz; they will forward them to us.

Your superior in painting,
ANDREY.

Bojidar :

Come to-morrow, Wednesday, at eleven o'clock. We are going to baptize Louis Snowball, as he receives his first communion on the day after to-morrow. The priest discovered that he had never been baptized. This seems to be an exaggeration, but it is the truth. Till to-morrow, then, without fail.

MARIE BASHKIRTSEFF.

If you cannot come, telegraph to-morrow before one o'clock.

www.ingramcontent.com/pod-product-compliance
Lightning Source LLC
Chambersburg PA
CBHW021942240426
43668CB00037B/425